AN INTRODUCTION
QUR'ANIC EXEGESIS
TAFSIR

MUHİTTİN AKGÜL

AN INTRODUCTION TO QUR'ANIC EXEGESIS
TAFSIR

MUHITTIN AKGÜL

TUGHRA
BOOKS
New Jersey

Translated by Zainab Mahmoud

Published by Tughra Books
345 Clifton Ave., Clifton,
NJ, 07011, USA

www.tughrabooks.com

Library of Congress Cataloging-in-Publication Data

Akgül, Muhittin.
[Tefsir. English]
An introduction to Qur'anic exegesis : tafsir / Muhittin Akgül.
pages cm
ISBN 978-1-59784-316-4 (alk. paper)
1. Qur'an--Criticism, interpretation, etc. 2. Qur'an--Hermeneutics. I. Title. II. Title: Tafsir.
BP130.1.A46513 2014
297.1'22601--dc23
2014036470

ISBN: 978-1-59784-316-4

Printed by
Çağlayan A.Ş., Izmir - Turkey

CONTENTS

UNIT 1
The Definition of the Qur'an

UNIT 2
The Definition of Revelation

UNIT 3
The Miraculousness of the Qur'an

UNIT 4
The Writing, Gathering and Copying of the Qur'an

UNIT 5
The Definition of *Surah* and *Ayah*

UNIT 6
Short Commentaries

UNIT 1

THE DEFINITION OF THE QUR'AN

THE DICTIONARY AND TERMINOLOGICAL
DEFINITIONS OF THE WORD "QUR'AN"

Before commencing onto the topics regarding the Holy Scripture, we should briefly study the actual meaning of the word "Qur'an." The dictionary meaning of the word Qur'an derives from the word "qara'a," and means to read. This subtly signifies that the Qur'an is the most widely read book on earth today and of the future.

The Qur'an;

1. is the Word of Allah.
2. was sent down to Prophet Muhammad, peace and blessings be upon him, by means of revelations.
3. is a miracle in its wording and meaning.
4. was conveyed by verbal perpetuation from generation to generation.
5. was compiled in written scripts (*mushaf*).
6. Its recitation is a form of worship.

We will study this in greater detail, but to explain this briefly:

1. The Qur'an was received by noble Prophet in the form of revelations over a period of twenty three years.
2. It is a miracle in its meaning and wording. In short, the Qur'an is unique and has its own specific approach, presentation and analysis of the issues and topics it addresses. Just as no human was capable of producing anything like it during that period or in later periods, no human will ever be capable of producing anything like it in the future.

3. The Qur'an was transmitted by verbal perpetuation from one entire generation to the next. In other words, it was transmitted by such a vast number of individuals that logically there was no possibility of any fabrication, and again being uninterruptedly transmitted by successive generations of such magnitude is evidence that there is no probability to the contrary.

4. These revelations from Surah al-Fatiha to Surah an-Nas were documented in written scripts. The plural of *mushaf* is *musahif*, meaning a compilation of written scripts in book form.

5. The Qur'an is a book whose recitation is a form of worship.

6. The Qur'an is the Word of Allah.

OTHER NAMES OF THE QUR'AN

The Qur'an has many names. But needless to say, the most commonly used name is "Qur'an." This is mentioned in the Qur'an: *"Most certainly it is a Qur'an (recited) most honorable"* (al-Waqiah 56:77)

1. Al-Kitab; meaning the Qur'an.

    This is the Book: there is no doubt about it. (al-Baqarah 2:1–2).

2. Al-Furqan; meaning the Criterion for right and wrong, it was given this title because it differentiates between the truth and false, the lawful and unlawful.

3. Adh-Dhikr; which means a reminder, to remember. The Qur'an was given this title because it is a reminder of Allah.

    Indeed it is We, We Who sent down the Reminder in parts, and it is indeed We Who are its Guardian (al-Hijr 15:9).

4. Al-Huda; meaning guidance. The Book of Allah was given this name because it guides the people to the path of truth.

    "…as guidance for the people…" (Al Imran 3:4).

THE VIRTUES OF READING THE QUR'AN IN THE CORRECT MANNER

In many of the hadiths, Prophet Muhammad, peace and blessings be upon him, related that reading the Qur'an in the correct manner and acting upon its commands is the means of great rewards from Allah. Here are just a few of those traditions (hadiths):

1. "The best of you is the one who learns the Qur'an and teaches it to others."

2. "Read the Qur'an, for verily it will come on the Day of Judgment as an intercessor for its companions."

3. "Those who recite the Qur'an beautifully will be with the noble scribes (angels). Those who read it with difficulty will obtain double the reward."

4. "Whoever reads a letter from the Book of Allah, he will have a reward, and that reward will be multiplied by ten. I am not saying that "Alif, Lam, Mim" is one letter, rather I am saying that "alif" is a letter, "lam" is a letter and "mim" is a letter."

5. "Whoever reads the Qur'an and acts upon what it contains, his parents shall be made to wear a crown, the light of which will be brighter than the sun that illuminates the world."

Points to Consider While Reading the Qur'an

1. The Qur'an must not be recited, read or touched while in a state of major impurity.

2. The Qur'an may be recited or read without performing the ablutions (*wudu*), however, reciting the Qur'an in the state of purification is more meritorious.

3. The recitation of the Qur'an should begin by proclaiming *A'udhu billahi min ash-shaytani'r-rajim* (I seek refuge in Allah from the Satan, the accursed one).

4. When reciting the Qur'an, each letter should be read distinctly and in the proper manner, without haste and in accordance to elocution of reciting the Holy Scripts.

5. The reciter must contemplate the meaning of the verses while reading.

6. These are not the words of humans, the Qur'an is the Word of Allah and therefore should be read with respect and submissiveness.

7. The area in which the Qur'an is recited must be clean.

8. The reciter must attempt to use the voice in the correct manner and be instructed regarding the recitation of the Qur'an.

9. Those who read the Qur'an should strive to act upon its commands.

10. The Qur'an must not be held below waist level.

IS IT POSSIBLE TO TRANSLATE THE QUR'AN LITERALLY?

Translation is to translate a word or text into another language. In addition to the great importance and many advantages of translations, it is extremely difficult to find words that convey the characteristics in the meaning of a word, and express these characteristics identically in another language. Although to a certain extent it may be possible to translate a text written in a plain term that addresses the mind and logic alone almost accurately, it is almost impossible to translate such a book or text containing the subtleties of literature and splendor into another language literally. Especially when the Book is the Holy Qur'an, a miracle in every aspect, it is impossible to translate and convey its exact meaning and splendor.

In these few paragraphs, we will attempt to give an explanation for the reasons why an exact translation is not possible:

Firstly, a language does not simply consist of an overall pattern of letters and words. The language of a nation is a reflection of the culture, character, history and the region in which that nation lives. The equivalent of any word in another language can never reflect the exact expression, and the effect it has on those who speak the original language.

For example: The meaning of the word "Qur'an" is "read." However, when we say "Qur'an," it is impossible to translate its entire meaning that comes to mind into another language in a single word. No word or infinitive in any other language, or for example the English words "reading" or "recitation," is an exact equivalent of the word Qur'an. A language is not a lifeless element, but is rather an expressive element which undergoes changes and adaptations together with the history of its users.

Secondly, Arabic is a totally grammatical language. Its principles are distinct, and are established. Particularly in terms of lexicalization, Arabic is the richest language in the world. For instance, in Arabic, there are 35 forms known as the infinitive pool, in other words 35 different infinitives are formed from one verb and each of these expresses a different meaning and connotation than the other.

To give another example: The past tense, present tense and future tense in one language are not always identical to those in other languages. For instance, in particular when the Qur'an mentions the facts and events of the Hereafter, it uses the simple present tense, whereas in terms of the history of humanity this is a forthcoming event. Such usage in the Qur'an, besides expressing the certainty of the past in Arabic, also has many other pretexts and expression of meaning.

THE DEFINITION, PURPOSE, SIGNIFICANCE AND VARIATIONS OF THE QUR'ANIC EXEGESIS

Definition of Exegesis (*Tafsir*): This is a branch of science which explains the Qur'an, the Book of Allah in a manner which people are able to understand.

The purpose of the Exegesis: The purpose of the exegesis is for the whole of humanity to comprehend and represent the Qur'an in the manner which pleases Allah so they attain happiness both in this world and the Hereafter, and gain the ability of earning the rewards of Allah.

The significance of the Exegesis: There is great reward in reciting the Qur'an, however reciting it alone is not sufficient. It is necessary to unveil this sublime treasure, to understand it and benefit from it. The key to that treasure is the exegesis. An exegesis or commentary is the only means of fully understanding the Qur'an, and the most important point is reading it with understanding. This is the measure of a Muslims progress or decline. During the periods in which the Qur'an was perceived and the people lived in accordance with the spirit and commands of the Qur'an, the Muslims prospered, and in the times when they acted contrary to the Qur'an, they made no progress. Indeed, the holy Qur'an was sent for the believers to understand it.

UNIT 2

THE DEFINITION OF REVELATION

THE DICTIONARY AND TERMINOLOGICAL DEFINITION OF THE WORD *WAHY* (REVELATION)

The dictionary definition of *wahy* (revelation): The way Allah sends His commands and prohibitions to His Messenger either directly or by means of an angel.

HOW THE REVELATIONS WERE SENT

As the Qur'an relates, Allah the Almighty speaks to humans in three different ways. He conveys His words into the hearts of people, speaks from behind a veil or speaks through an angel. This is conveyed in the Qur'an in these words:

> It is not for any mortal that Allah should speak to him unless it be by Revelation or from behind a veil, or by sending a messenger (angel) to reveal, by His leave, whatever He wills. (ash-Shuara 53:51)

Generally this is how revelations are sent. However, when we study the forms in which the revelations were sent to Prophet Muhammad, peace and blessings be upon him, we see that this was a little more detailed.

1. The revelations were sent in forms of good dreams. The dreams of the noble Prophet were as clear as light.
2. When he was awake, Jibril (the Archangel Gabriel) conveyed the revelations into the heart of the Prophet.
3. The Divine revelations were conveyed by an angel. The Angel of Revelation, Jibril, appeared as both a human and in his own form.

4. The Angel of revelation conveyed the Holy Scripts in the sound of a ringing bell. This was the most difficult form of receiving the revelations for the Prophet.

5. Allah the Almighty addressed the Prophet directly. This occurred on the night of ascendance.

6. Jibril came with the holy revelations while the Prophet was sleeping. The Angel would convey the Divine commands into the Prophet's heart when he was asleep.

THE BEGINNING OF THE REVELATIONS, THE DATE AND THE PROPHET'S SPIRITUAL STATE DURING THIS PROCESS

The people of Mecca were living in a state of disbelief and polytheism, and were engrossed in falsehood and corruption as in the case of those like Abu Jahl and Abu Lahab. The heart of one among these people had remained pure from the whirlpool of superstition and falsehoods. The Divine Mercy had protected him. His heart was constantly beating for the people, he continuously contemplated how they could escape the deviation and reach salvation, how they could abandon idol worshipping. On certain days, the Prophet would go to the cave of Hira, where he would sit in a state of meditation and worship. On yet another of his visits to the cave, as he was about to leave the Prophet heard a voice as if it was echoing from a distance. The voice was clear and distinct: "Read!"

The Prophet replied: "I do not know how to read."

The voice repeated: "Read!"

And after the third time, when the Prophet asked, "What shall I read?" the voice grew louder:

> Read in, and with the Name of your Lord, Who has created. Created human from a clot clinging (to the wall of the womb). Read, and your Lord is the All-Munificent, Who has taught (human) by the pen. Taught human what he did not know. (al-Alaq 96:1–4)

The Prophet repeated the words, then he returned home shaking with fear and told his dear wife Khadija, "Cover me, cover me!"

He remained beneath the covers until his fear passed, then what happened after was related by Khadija: "Rejoice and be cheerful. He in Whose hands stands Khadija's life bears witness to the truth that you will be the Prophet to this people."

Khadija told the Prophet to rest, and went to visit her cousin Waraqa ibn Nawfal. Waraqa, who was now old and blind, had great knowledge of the Torah and the Bible, and after listening to Khadija, he replied: "I swear by Allah that the same spirit, the Angel of revelation who descended to Prophet Musa, peace be upon him, has descended unto him, and no doubt he is the Prophet of these people, of the people. Tell him to remain strong. If only I would be alive when they drive him out of his homeland, I would give him all my support."

Khadija, the Prophet's dear wife returned home in a state of excitement and explained what Waraqa had told her. The Prophet praise his Lord.

The Date: The first revelation was received by the Prophet at the age of forty years old, on Monday 17th Ramadan in the year 610 CE.

The Qur'an was sent down in its entirety from the Supreme Preserved Tablet to the heavens of this world, and was then sent down to the noble Prophet in stages.

THE FIRST VERSE REVEALED, THE INTERREGNUM ERA AND THE LAST VERSE OF THE QUR'AN REVEALED

The first verses of the Qur'an to be revealed were the first five verses of chapter al-Alaq. These verses affirmed the tidings of Prophethood, but the Prophet had not yet been given the command to convey this. Following these first revelations, there was an interval between the revelations which lasted around forty days, and this is known as the interregnum era. Then the revelations continued. The revelations which followed were:

> O, you cloaked one! Arise and warn! And declare your Lord's greatness! And keep your clothing clean! Keep away from all pollution; Do not consider your fulfillment of these orders as a kindness; And for the sake of your Lord, be patient. (al-Muddathir 74:1–7)

The first five verses of Surah al-Alaq affirmed the Prophethood of Prophet Muhammad, peace and blessings be upon him, and the first seven verses of Surah al-Muddathir following the interregnum era, affirmed him as a Messenger of Allah.

The last revelation was sent nine days before the death of the Prophet:

> And guard yourselves against a Day in which you will be brought back to Allah. Then every soul will be repaid in full what it has earned (while in the world), and they will not be wronged. (al-Baqarah 2:281)

THE CHARACTERISTICS OF THE MECCAN AND MEDINAN VERSES

A majority of the verses regarding the obligatory duties and Islamic laws were Medinan, whereas the Meccan verses place more of an emphasis on the foundation of religion and the principles of faith based on unification. These revelations were aimed at destroying polytheism and engrossing the hearts with good morals, as the people were practicing idolatry during the first years of Prophethood, an era in which both ignorance and deviation were at a peak.

The verses beginning with "O humankind" are Meccan verses.

And those which begin "O you who believe" are Medinan verses.

The Meccan surahs are short and bear an intense spirit of struggle, whereas the Medinan surahs are usually longer. In the Meccan surahs of the Qur'an, there are stories and examples of past communities, and it commands "Learn a lesson" from this.

The Medinan surahs mention topics such as the obligatory duties, punishments and worship.

The Jews and Christians are not mentioned in the Meccan surahs due to the struggle during that period. The Jews, Christians and hypocrites are mentioned in the Medinan surahs.

There is no mention of jihad in the Meccan surahs, but rather there is the call to faith, conveying the message and warning, whereas the Medinan surahs speak of jihad.

There are 1,456 verses which are Medinan, and the remaining verses were revealed during the Meccan period.

THE WISDOM OF THE QUR'AN'S REVELATION IN STAGES

1. The Qur'an instituted a huge transformation never witnessed before throughout the world's history, and established unprecedented order. The principles and commands of the Qur'an were sent in stages so the people could gradually adapt to these changes.

   It would have been impossible for the people who lived during the period of ignorance to suddenly abandon the bad principles and habits they were accustomed to. Indeed, this would have been extremely difficult for humans by nature.

   If the first command to those addicted to alcohol was to give up drinking, they would quite likely have objected or ignored the command.

   The Qur'an placed an emphasis on the people reaching a certain level of maturity and ascribed its commands in a gentle, gradual manner.

2. Additionally, as the revelations were sent, the Companions memorized the scripts and contemplated their meaning. At the same time, they were personally executing each of these commands. If the entire Qur'an was sent down at one time, understanding and applying these commands would have become extremely difficult.

3. The revelation of the Divine Scripts in stages was a great source of joy both to the Prophet and to the Muslims of that period. Under

the oppression and hostility of their adversaries, the revelations were a source of consolation; it raised their spirits, they became even stronger and attained new dynamism.

4. Another reason for the revelations being sent in stages was to eliminate the disbeliever's conception that "This was previously devised and written by humans."

5. Finally; many of the verses of the Qur'an were clearly sent in connection with a specific question or event during that period. Therefore, it was quite natural for the revelations to be sent over a period of time.

UNIT 3

THE MIRACULOUSNESS OF THE QUR'AN

THE FIRST STEP: "WE CAN CALL IT SORCERY."

Following the interregnum era, once again the revelations of guidance and light began to ascend. During the fourth year of Prophethood, after the secret call to faith which lasted almost three years, the numbers embracing Islam began to increase. This alarmed the polytheists immensely, they did not know what to do.

Whenever the noble Prophet meets the members of the Quraysh, he would recite the Qur'an and mention the Name of Allah. The members of the Quraysh were enchanted by the melodious tone and gentle sound of the Qur'an, so the disobedient ones covered their ears so they would not hear its recitation.

The leaders of the Quraysh meet frequently, they spoke about the Prophet and the revelations that were sent to him and tried to find a way to prevent the people from listening to the recitation of the Holy Scripts.

On one occasion, they meet yet again, one of the leaders said "What was revealed to him was magic." One of the others said "This is not magic this is poetry," and another of the leaders said "This is neither magic nor poetry, it is soothsaying."

Walid ibn Mughira joined the argument "If you say he is possessed, he has no signs of being possessed, if you say he is a soothsayer, we have seen soothsayers, If you say he poet, we know poetry in all forms. By Allah, his speech is so sweet that whatever you say will be in vain. The nearest thing to the truth is saying he is a sorcerer." The Hajj season had arrived, and the Prophet would stand on the roadside reciting the Qur'an and declaring the Word of Allah in an attempt of inviting the envoys to Islam. The Quraysh continuously followed the Prophet, and whenever he began to convey the Word of Allah to the Arabs who came from afar, they would immediately surround him and warn the Arabs to ignore him and not be influenced by his words of magic.

However, when Allah wills, He creates the means and nothing can prevent this from happening.

As a result of these acts of sabotage the Qurayshi leaders resorted to attempting to prevent the people from listening to the Qur'an, this induced their curiosity and led them to show even greater interest in the Prophet's words. These groups began to convey the Qur'an and Islam, and before long news of the Messenger of Allah had spread throughout the entire Arabian Peninsula. The people were speaking of the arrival of the Prophet in every corner of the region. The result of the hypocrite's objectives was much different than they had previously anticipated.

ALL KINDS OF OPPRESSIONS AND BOYCOTTS

The activities aimed at preventing the conveyance of the Qur'an were not limited to this alone, but they also resorted to many forms of oppression and persecution never even dreamt of. Many, including Bilal al-Habashi, Ammar ibn Yasir, Suhayb ar-Rumi, and from among the women Nahdiyah and Umm Abis were subjected to persecution. While the Prophet was praying in the mosque, Uqba threw the intestines of a camel onto his back. In view of these events, the Muslims initially considered migrating to Abyssinia, thus the migration to Abyssinia began.

Abu Bakr set out on the journey, and on the way he met Ibn ad-Daghina. Ibn ad-Daghina asked Abu Bakr where he was heading, he replied: "The Quraysh have driven me out of my homeland, I am going to a place where I can worship my Lord in peace and liberty."

Ibn ad-Daghina said: "You are a worthy, honorable man who respects his family, helps the poor and destitute, entertains his guests generously," and told Abu Bakr to return to his homeland and remain in Mecca.

The Quraysh agreed on the condition that Abu Bakr abstained from reciting the Qur'an in public.

Abu Bakr continued to recite the Qur'an in a room of his house. When the women and younger members of the society began to abandon the belief of their forefathers on hearing Abu Bakr's recitation of the Qur'an, the polytheists went to Ibn ad-Daghina and complained in an attempt of silencing the Book of Allah.

On another occasion, Abdullah ibn Mas'ud was beaten by the polytheists until his face was bruised and covered in blood for reciting the Qur'an aloud in the Ka'ba.

This is generally how the days passed, however, the Quraysh's oppression towards the Muslims was increasing with every passing day.

Powerful and highly respected men such as Abu Bakr, Hamza and Umar embracing Islam alarmed the Quraysh immensely, and in 617 CE they declared a boycott against the families of Hashim and Muttalib, they were to cease the establishment of family ties, they were not to exchange their daughters in marriage or trade with these two families. An extremely difficult three years passed, and eventually the boycott ended in 619 CE.

In 620 CE the Prophet travelled to Taif in the hope of conveying Islam, but nobody listened to his call. The habitants of the city stoned the Prophet until he was covered in blood, and he departed from the city in a state of grief.

THE LEADERS OF THE QURAYSH LISTENED TO THE RECITATION OF THE QUR'AN IN SECRET

While the Prophet was praying at home one night, the leading figures of the polytheists such as Abu Sufyan, Abu Jahl and Ahnas, stood hidden in the darkness and listened to the recitation of the Qur'an. Unaware of one another's presence, they were so absorbed in the Prophet's recitation that they remained there until dawn. As they were about to leave at dawnbreak, the three men noticed one another. Each began to condemn the other for listening to the Qur'an, and agreed not to do such a thing again saying that this would certainly raise suspicion and doubt if they were seen by others.

But this happened again the next day, and on the third consecutive day the three men said "We cannot continue doing this!" so each of them vowed not to go there again.

Clearly, the hearts were unable to escape from the delightful, fascinating effects of the Qur'an. However, aspects such as tribal ties, personal vengeance, the battle for leadership and jealousy was preventing them from embracing Islam.

UMAR IN THE PRESENCE OF THE QUR'AN

Umar related his acceptance of Islam in these words:

I was one of the most brutal men towards the Messenger of Allah. As I was walking through the streets of Mecca one day, I came across a member of the Quraysh. He asked, "Where are you going?" I told him where I was heading and he remarked; you consider yourself to be so strong, but this issue has even entered your own home!

I asked: "What are you talking about?"

He replied: "You should put you own family in order first, your sister and her husband are following the religion of Muhammad."

I returned home in a state of anger. Whenever a person embraced Islam, the Prophet would assign one or two of the believers to teach this person the Islamic faith. There were two people in my sister's house, they were reciting the Qur'an. I went to her house and knocked on the door. When she asked "Who is it" from behind the door, I replied: "The son of Khattab."

My sister opened the door, and the other two women hid in another room. I asked her:

They told me that you abandoned you faith, is this true? And I struck her.

Her mouth was bleeding, she replied: "You hit me because we accept religion of truth? Yes we are Muslims, so do whatever you consider fit."

I noticed some pages in the corner and asked "What are those scripts? Show them to me." But she would not give them to me until I had purified myself saying the scripts were not to be touched in a state of impurity. So I purified myself and took the pages, it wrote: *"Whatever is in the heavens and the earth glorifies Allah…"* (al-Hadid 57:1).

I continued to read, and proclaiming the following words "I declare there is no deity but Allah and I declare that Muhammad is the servant and Messenger of Allah" (*Ash hadu anla ilaha illallah wa ash hadu anna Muhammadan abduhu wa Rasuluhu*), I became a Muslim. According to reports, the surah of the Qur'an recited was Surah Ta-Ha. Indeed, reading a few verses of the Qur'an even softened the heart of a man as stern as Umar, and encouraged him to embrace Islam.

UNIT 4

THE WRITING, GATHERING AND COPYING OF THE QUR'AN

THE PERIOD OF THE MESSENGER OF ALLAH: THE WRITING OF THE QUR'AN

At the time when the first revelations began, the Messenger of Allah had no knowledge regarding the revelation of the Divine Scripts. In the fear that he may forget what was revealed to him, the Prophet attempted to repeat the sections of the verses which had already been sent before the revelation ended. Thereupon the following verse was revealed:

> (O Prophet!) Move not your tongue to hasten it. Surely it is for Us to collect it(in your heart) and enable you to recite it (by heart). So when We recite it, follow its recitation; Thereafter, it is for Us to explain it. (al-Qiyamah 75:16–19)

From these verses, we can clearly see that Allah the Almighty guaranteed three points from the very beginning:

1. Gathering it in the heart as required,
2. Reciting it in the most favorable manner,
3. Accuracy in recitation and explanation.

Since the very beginning the Qur'an was preserved by the following three methods:

1. Written scripts: Following the warnings defined above and his experiences, the Prophet had attained sufficient knowledge regarding the mechanism of revelation. He would previously sense that a revelation was to be sent, and would call a scribe to write down the revelations. Almost forty of the Companions were honored to be scribes of the revelations, however among them Zayd ibn Thabit was given

the title *Al-Katib* (The Scribe) because he was the one who recorded the most revelations.

One thing that we should empathize at this point, is that there
was no previously known date or time for the forthcoming of the
revelations. Therefore, the Prophet was prepared at all times. Even
during the migration, the most difficult stage of his Prophethood, he
ensured that there was a scriber and writing material with him at all
times.

In fact, on the military expeditions the Prophet would have the
scripts written during rests on the journey, and when the scriber fin-
ished, he would repeat it to the Prophet and correct any mistakes.

2. Memorization of the Qur'an: The Companions, and initially the
scribers immediately memorized the revelations as they were sent
and these verses were recited at least five times a day during the
Prescribed Prayers. Although we cannot say all of the revelations
were memorized by each of the believers, a vast majority certainly
did learn them by heart.

3. Revision or public recitation (*ardan*): In view of the possibility of un-
intended mistakes during the stages of writing and memorizing the
Qur'an, the Prophet eliminated any likelihood of this by taking a
third measure. This is called the *Ardan* Method (revision); this
means the process of controlling the written scripts by listening to
someone who had memorized the scripts. This is how it was done:
Every Ramadan the Prophet would recite the revelations sent during the period between the previous Ramadan to Jibril, and then
before the congregation in the Masjid an-Nabawi (the Prophet's
Mosque) so the people could control their written scripts and verses
they had memorized. This was carried out twice during the last year
before the Prophet's death, this was known as *ard al-ahir*.

However, the question 'was there a need for such frequent control when the Qur'an was under Divine security?' may come to
mind. This is true, the preservation of the Qur'an was guaranteed,

but we can say this was practiced as an assurance for the future generations who could doubt the authenticity of the Qur'an due to their weakness in faith, and to eliminate any apprehensions regarding the subject.

Therefore, this practice is objective evidence for both believers and disbelievers regarding the authenticity in the compilation process of the scriptures during the period of the Prophet, and after his death.

THE PERIOD OF ABU BAKR: THE GATHERING OF THE QUR'AN

At the time of the Prophet's death, although the entire Qur'an had been written, these scriptures had not yet been compiled into book form. This was due to the fact that the Prophet had no knowledge of when the revelations were to cease. However, as a result of the spread of Islam to other regions, many of the Companions migrated and settled in various other places following the death of the Prophet. In the battle of Yamama against Musaylama, a liar who claimed to be a prophet, almost seventy Companions who were memorizers of the Qur'an were killed. The Companions were afraid that the scripts written during the time of the Prophet would be lost, so on the suggestion of Umar, Caliph Abu Bakr gathered the most prominent of the Companions at Umar's home. At this meeting, the Companions established the principles of gathering the Qur'an, and decided to assign Zayd ibn Thabit to fulfill this task.

Zayd ibn Thabit was an intelligent, honorable and learned person, a man of virtue who was one of the Prophet's scribers who had written the revelations. He established a committee of which the prominent Companions such as Uthman, Ali, Abdullah ibn Mas'ud were members. The committee only accepted scripts that were testified by two witnesses as being written as dictated identically by the Prophet in their presence. On completion of this extremely important task, Umar gathered the Companions and recited the verses all of which were then acknowledged and approved by all the Companions. Thus, the entire Qur'an had been collected during the period of Caliph Abu Bakr.

THE PERIOD OF UTHMAN: THE COPYING OF THE QUR'AN

During the period of Caliph Uthman, the Islamic state expanded, and the numbers of Muslims were increasing daily. Teachers of the Qur'an were sent to the settlements within the Islamic state. These teachers taught the recitation in their own particular style. This caused controversy among the people who were unaware that the Qur'an could be read in different styles of recitation.

Explanation: During the first years of Prophethood, the Arab tribes who spoke with a different dialect were permitted to recite the Qur'an according to the seven letters (*qira'at*) to make the transition process until they learned the Qurayshi dialect easier.

In an attempt of ending this controversy, Caliph Uthman sent for the Qur'an that was compiled during the period of Abu Bakr, and classifying these as the original scripts, ordered the copying of the Qur'an.

A committee comprising of Abdullah ibn Zubayr, Said ibn al-As and Abdullah ibn Harith was established and headed by Zayd ibn Thabit. The manuscripts of the Qur'an copied by this committee were sent to each of the Muslim cities, and the original copy of the Qur'an was returned to Hafsa, the Prophet's dear wife. The original copy of the Qur'an remained in the holy city of Medina, and the seven copies were sent to major cities such as Kufa, Basra, Damascus, Mecca, Egypt, Yemen and Bahrain.

Over a period of time, the numbers of these Qur'ans were increased.

UNIT 5

THE DEFINITION OF
SURAH AND AYAH

THE DEFINITION OF THE WORD "SURAH" (CHAPTER), THE SEQUENCE AND NUMBER OF CHAPTERS IN THE QUR'AN

The technical term of the word *surah* is the title given to each individual division or chapter of the Qur'an. Surah as a word can also mean rank, honor, position and sign. The plural of surah is "Suwar." It is mentioned nine times in the Qur'an.

The order of the surahs was compiled on the personal command of the Prophet. He informed the revelation scribers of where each of the surahs should be placed. The gathering of the scripts, and the scripts being compiled into book form again was executed on the command of the Prophet. The memorizers had already learned the order of the Qur'an, as every Ramadan Jibril and the Prophet recited the Qur'an to one another in this order, and then the Prophet would publically recite this to the Companions. In addition, the Qur'an was recited according to this order during the Prayers.

In total there are 114 surahs in the Qur'an. The names of each of these surahs were dictated by the noble Prophet himself.

THE DEFINITION OF THE WORD "AYAH" (VERSE), THE SEQUENCE AND NUMBER OF VERSES IN THE QUR'AN

The meaning of the word "ayah" is miracle, a sign or evidence. The terminological meaning of the word "ayah" is a revelation comprising of one or more sentences. The order of the ayahs, the beginning, end, and instruction of which ayahs belonged to which surah was again related personally by the noble Prophet.

According to general opinion, the number of ayahs is 6,666. However, although different figures may be obtained according to the principles of counting, the majority opinion regarding the number of ayahs is 6,236.

THE VOWEL SIGNS AND DIACRITICAL MARKS

In the same way that there were no vowel signs and diacritical points on the scripts gathered during the period of Caliph Abu Bakr, there were no vowel signs or diacritical points in the Qur'an that were copied and sent to the major Islamic cities during the period of Uthman, because the vowel signs and diacritical points were not used in the Arab Peninsula at that time. As the Companions and believers of that period learnt the Qur'an by ear, everyone recited the Qur'an correctly in the way they had heard and been taught, therefore there was no question of the Qur'an being recited incorrectly.

However, as the boundaries of the Islamic state expanded and the Arabs began to mix with the languages and cultures of other nations, certain changes emerged in Arabic lettering. The non-Arabs found it difficult to read the Qur'an without any vowel signs and diacritical marks. Therefore the practice of using diacritical marks began when Zayd, the governor of Basra informed Abu al- Aswad al-Du'ali, a man who had great knowledge in the field of Arabic of this request. In that period this was done by placing a dot above the letter instead of the *fatha* (a small diagonal line above the letter), a dot below the letter rather than the *kasra* (a diagonal line below the letter), a dot in front of the letter instead of the *dhamma* (a small curl like sign above the letter) and two dots rather than the *sukun* (a small circle above the letter).

Later in 791, the diacritical and vowel signs we are familiar with today were introduced by Khalil ibn Ahmad al-Farahidi.

The decorative signs indicating the beginning of a surah, the circles that signify the end of a verse and the marks indicating the different sections of the Qur'an were all introduce in later periods.

UNIT 6

SHORT COMMENTARIES

SURAH AL-FATIHA

بِسْمِ اللهِ الرَّحْمٰنِ الرَّحِيمِ ۞ اَلْحَمْدُ لِلهِ رَبِّ الْعَالَمِينَ ۞ اَلرَّحْمٰنِ الرَّحِيمِ ۞
مَالِكِ يَوْمِ الدِّينِ ۞ إِيَّاكَ نَعْبُدُ وَإِيَّاكَ نَسْتَعِينُ ۞ اِهْدِنَا الصِّرَاطَ الْمُسْتَقِيمَ ۞
صِرَاطَ الَّذِينَ أَنْعَمْتَ عَلَيْهِمْ غَيْرِ الْمَغْضُوبِ عَلَيْهِمْ وَلاَ الضَّالِّينَ ۞

Interpretation

1. In the Name of Allah, the All-Merciful, the All-Compassionate,
2. All praise and gratitude are for Allah, the Lord of the worlds,
3. The All-Merciful, the All-Compassionate,
4. The Master of the Day of Judgment.
5. You alone do we worship, and from You alone do we seek help.
6. Guide us to the Straight Path,
7. The Path of those whom You have favored, not of those who have incurred Your wrath, nor of those who are astray.

Names of the surah

Surah al-Fatiha has various names. The Qur'an refers to this surah as the seven oft or doubly repeated verses (*Sab'a al-Masani*) because it is repeated in the Prayers. Additionally, the Prophet referred to this surah as The Mother of the Book (*Ummu'l-Kitab*) because it is the essence of the Qur'an, The Healer (*Ash-Shifa*) because it is a cure for both physical and spiritual diseases, and The Opener (*Al-Fatiha*) because the Prayers and the Qur'an begin with this surah.

Virtues of al-Fatiha

According to a report by Abu Hurayra, Allah the Almighty speaks with His servant in Surah al-Fatiha: "Allah the Almighty has said: 'I have divided Surah al-Fatiha between Myself and My servant into two halves, and My servant shall have what he has asked for. When the servant says, الْحَمْدُ لله رَبّ الْعَالَمِينَ "All praise and gratitude are for Allah, the Lord of the worlds" Allah the Almighty says: 'My servant has praised Me.' When he says, الرَّحْمٰنِ الرَّحِيم "The All-Merciful, the All-Compassionate," Allah the Almighty says: 'My servant has extolled Me.' When he says, مَالِكِ يَوْم الدّين "The Master of the Day of Judgment," Allah the Almighty says: 'My servant has glorified Me,' and when he says, إِيَّاكَ نَعْبُدُ وَإِيَّاكَ نَسْتَعِينُ "You alone do we worship, and from You alone do we seek help," He says: 'This is between Me and My servant, and My servant shall have what he has asked for.'"

Abu Said al-Khudri related: "We were on a journey, we stopped to rest for a while. A person came and said 'The leader of our tribe has been stung by a scorpion. Our men are not present, is there anyone among you who can treat him?' One of the men went and recited Surah al-Fatiha. The leader of the tribe recovered. The tribe gave him thirty sheep and gave us some of the milk to drink. We asked him, 'Did you know how to cure?' He replied 'No, I cured him by reciting al-Fatiha.' We warned him 'Do not touch what they gave you without asking the Messenger of Allah first!' When he came to Medina, we told the Prophet what had happened. He replied, 'How did you know that Surah al-Fatiha was a cure? Take what they gave you and keep a share for me!'"

Surah al-Fatiha is indeed a Divine treasure. It beholds the cure for the suffering of the aggrieved. It is the first surah of the Qur'an. Thus, there is no surah prior to it, thus the reason why everything begins with Surah al-Fatiha.

There is a close relationship between "Bismillahir Rahmanir Rahim" and al-Fatiha. "Bismillah" is in a sense a verse from al-Fatiha. This is why many of the Islamic scholars classify "Bismillah" as one of the seven verses of Surah al-Fatiha." There is a kind of poetical harmony between "Bismillah" and al-Fatiha. "Bismillah" begins in the Name of Allah. In the same way that we begin reciting of the Qur'an in the Name of Allah, we also begin the recitation of al-Fatiha proclaiming "Bismillah." Indeed, any deeds or tasks that begin without reciting the Name of Allah are incomplete.

اَلْحَمْدُ لِلهِ رَبِّ الْعَالَمِينَ Surah al-Fatiha begins with the word "Praise." As a word, although this means glorification and gratitude, there is a difference. This is why Surah al-Fatiha begins with اَلْحَمْدُ لِلهِ, rather than اَلشُّكْرُ لِلهِ or اَلْمَدْحُ لِلهِ.

Praise is the general denotation of gratitude towards the blessings of Allah whether they reach us or not, whether we perceive, if we are aware of these blessings or not. Therefore, such a word can be used to convey gratitude for the Divine blessings in general.

Gratitude is our thanks for the blessings we perceive to the One Who bestows these favors.

Glorification means to exalt and praise. Allah is glorified due to His kindness and beauty, "O Lord! You are the possessor of beauty and kindness" is classified as praise. This can also be used to praise inanimate things such as trees and sustenance. Sometimes praise can be used in unnecessary instances, for example to flatter others. This is why we express our emotions of gratitude and praise to Allah with glorification.

The Prophet said: اَلْحَمْدُ رَأْسُ الشُّكْرِ "Praise is the major means of thanking Allah." If we are blessed with the favor of Allah or not, praise, in terms of turning towards Allah and sincerely expressing our emotions of gratefulness in a sense is superior to gratification.

The station of praise is an extremely important position, and this is why this is called "Al-Maqam al-Mahmud" or the Station of Praise. We supplicate to Allah following the *adhan* (call to Prayer) "O Lord! Raise him (Your Messenger) to the station of praise which You promised him."

The habitants of Paradise will enter saying:

دَعْوَاهُمْ فِيهَا سُبْحَانَكَ اللَّهُمَّ وَتَحِيَّتُهُمْ فِيهَا سَلَامٌ وَآخِرُ دَعْوَاهُمْ أَنِ الْحَمْدُ لِلهِ رَبِّ الْعَالَمِينَ

"All-Glorified You are, O Allah!" and their greeting will be: "Peace!" and *their invocation will close with 'All praise and gratitude are for Allah, the Lord of the worlds!'"* (Yunus 10:10).

The Messenger of Allah said: اَلْحَمْدُ لِلهِ تَمْلَأُ الْمِيزَانَ "Praising Allah fills the scales."

So what do we give praise and gratification for? That we are humans, we are believers, that Muhammad is our Prophet, that we are addressed by a universal Book such as the Qur'an, or for the blessings that we are, or are not aware of.

"Allah" means the One from whom everything is sought, the One who helps those in difficulty, the only One who is worshipped and the Giver of peace.

Lord (Rabb): Literally means the One Who disciplines. Allah is the One Who creates everything. He is the Creator, Provider, Trainer, Upbringer, and Director of all creatures. Allah is the One Who sends the Prophets and encourages complying with them, Who presents the principles of the Qur'an, Who awakens and stimulates the souls of humans, Who speaks of the universe in the Qur'an, Who describes the universe and clearly exhibits the truths before human beings.

Allah is the One Who raises the whole of existence, and every existence is raised within the boundaries of its own disposition. Indeed, the sole possessor of universal discipline is Allah, the Lord of the universe.

اَلرَّحْمنِ الرَّحِيم The All-Merciful (Ar-Rahman) and The All-Compassionate (Ar-Ŕahim) are two Names of Allah. Allah the Almighty describes Himself as Ar-Rahman and Ar-Rahim at the beginning of one hundred and thirteen surahs of the Qur'an, and in one of the verses of an-Naml. Ar-Rahman signifies forgiveness, compassion and the bestowal of sustenance which includes all, both believers and disbelievers. According to this, Allah grants blessings irrelevant of the people's faith, and does not deprive anyone of the environment in which they are able to live. In these terms, if Allah was not the Owner of this attribute, it would certainly have been impossible for the disbelievers to obtain a mouthful of water to drink in this world, whereas the attribute Ar-Rahim will manifest in the Hereafter rather than in this world.

مَالِكِ يَوْمِ الدِّينِ "Malik" means the Sovereign, the Owner. In other words, the sole Owner of the day of reward and punishment is Allah. Therefore, all other sovereigns are transient. It is virtually as if Allah is conveying a warning in this verse of the Qur'an: "O Pharaohs and Nimrods of this world, O those who boast of being rulers and show off, O kings… kings of kings! The day will come when the wealth and sovereignty you possess will disappear, and the sole Owner of that day will be Allah."

إِيَّاكَ نَعْبُدُ وَإِيَّاكَ نَسْتَعِينُ Servitude is being systematically respectful and submissive before Allah. Whereas worship; is the humans obedience anticipating affinity with Allah and anticipating reward with pure intention.

إِيَّاكَ نَعْبُدُ In these words there is clear indication that servitude is to Allah alone, and by saying إِيَّاكَ at the same time if the servant is engrossed in heedlessness or follows the devil, he will compose himself and remember Allah. Again, by saying this, the individual is in fact declaring to Whom he will practice servitude from the very beginning.

Saying "us" rather than "me" is giving Muslims social awareness, and indicates that the Prayers should be performed in congregation.

وَإِيَّاكَ نَسْتَعِينُ "…*from You alone do we seek help.*" In this there is seeing the help of Allah in everything we do, the request for performing worship with ease and aspiring His help in all we do. Since Allah has taught us to ask, this means He will give. When saying وَإِيَّاكَ نَسْتَعِينُ , by declaring that help is from Allah alone, the servant has reached the sincerity in his servitude. After saying إِيَّاكَ نَعْبُدُ "*You alone do we worship,*" again we seek refuge with وَإِيَّاكَ نَسْتَعِينُ "…*from You alone do we seek help.*"

Isti'ana means being dependent on Allah's help in all matters, asking Allah to grant us ease in performing worship and in the general issues humans face.

اهْدِنَا الصِّرَاطَ الْمُسْتَقِيمَ "*Guide us to the Straight Path.*" Allah is advising us to ask Him to guide us towards the path of truth. Indeed, how could an individual establish order in his personal, social or family life without the guidance of Allah? As indeed, all of this depends on Allah's guidance.

Guidance is the response of Allah to those in state of destitution that will suffice all their needs. The word اهد "ihdi" in Arabic means awaiting command. It means "Guide us, guide us to reaching faith." Occasionally, although all the means exist for this guidance, a person may not attain faith.

While the son of Nuh (Noah), who, although he was born and raised in the home of a Prophet was not blessed with faith, Ibrahim (Abraham) who was raised in the house of Azar, and Musa (Moses) who was born and raised in the home of the Pharaoh grew up and each became great Prophets. In one of his supplications, the Messenger of Allah prayed "O Lord! I ask You for guidance, piety and self-sufficiency" and by doing this was instructing us to ask this from Allah.

اَلصِّرَاطَ "As-sirat" means a certain path or road. This means a path that millions of righteous believers, thousands of Prophets and hundreds of thousands of companions of Allah have followed before us; or a wide path upon which everyone can walk.

اَلصِّرَاطَ الْمُسْتَقِيمَ This means the middle or moderate path, the path of truth, the path of Islamic jurisprudence, of Islam, the path of the Messenger of Allah and the Companions, the path to Paradise, the bridge over Hell.

When a servant says: اهْدِنَا الصِّرَاطَ الْمُسْتَقِيمَ "*Guide us to the Straight Path,*" this means O Lord! Sustain my faith and guidance, secure Your entrustment, my faith until I die, grant me success in retuning Your entrustment to You as a sound believer.

صِرَاطَ الَّذِينَ أَنْعَمْتَ عَلَيْهِمْ "*The path of those whom You have favored.*" In'am means an individual benefitting from and experiencing the bestowal of favors. Allah bestows blessings, and we obtain pleasure and enjoy these blessings. This is what we call *in'am*, and undoubtedly the greatest blessing of all is Islam.

We cannot bestow blessings, kings or rulers cannot bestow blessings. Only the true Owner of favors, of Sovereignty, the One who holds the power of commanding everything can bestow favors. The path of those referred to in the verse صِرَاطَ الَّذِينَ أَنْعَمْتَ عَلَيْهِمْ, and as defined in verse sixty nine of Surah an-Nisa is the path of the Prophets, the truthful ones, the witnesses, the righteous ones and the martyrs.

غَيْرِ الْمَغْضُوبِ عَلَيْهِمْ *Ghayr* means completely the opposite. Wrath means becoming angry, severity, displaying harshness and fury. So when we say غَيْرِ الْمَغْضُوب, this is portraying the meaning "not the path of those who su - fered the destruction of Allah or were subjected to the trial of Allah."

As for the word الضَّآلِّينَ; in Arabic, ضَلَالٌ "dalal" means deviation or going astray. "Dall" means a deviant person. الضَّآلِّينَ "Ad-dallin" is the plural meaning deviant people. "Dalalat" means heedlessness, not using the mind or being in a state of bewilderment. Therefore, when we say غَيْرِ الْمَغْضُوب عَلَيْهِمْ وَلَا الضَّآلِّينَ, we are asking Allah not to cast us onto the path of those in a state of bewilderment, those who are heedless to the clear scenes of truth and justice.

Again, these words refer to all those who deviated from the path of truth, and all those who were subjected to the wrath of Allah, so when we recite this, we are expressing that we seek the guidance of Allah from straying to the path the deviant one choose.

In one of his traditions, the Prophet said:

إِذَا أَمَّنَ الْإِمَامُ فَأَمِّنُوا فَإِنَّهُ مَنْ وَافَقَ تَأْمِينُهُ تَأْمِينَ الْمَلَائِكَةِ غُفِرَ لَهُ مَا تَقَدَّمَ مِنْ ذَنْبِهِ "When the imam says 'Amin,' then you should all say 'Amin,' for the angels say 'Amin' at that time, and he whose 'Amin' coincides with the 'Amin' of the angels, all his past sins will be forgiven."

آمِينَ "Amin" means "Accept our prayers." Therefore, by reciting al-Fat - ha we are displaying our servitude, asking for our needs and as a result of these appeals, we say "Amin" which means "Accept our requests."

SURAH AL-ASR

بِسْمِ اللهِ الرَّحْمٰنِ الرَّحِيمِ

وَالْعَصْرِ ۞ إِنَّ الْإِنْسَانَ لَفِي خُسْرٍ ۞ إِلَّا الَّذِينَ آمَنُوا وَعَمِلُوا

الصَّالِحَاتِ وَتَوَاصَوْا بِالْحَقِّ وَتَوَاصَوْا بِالصَّبْرِ ۞

Interpretation

In the Name of Allah, the All-Merciful, the All-Compassionate,

1. By time,

2. Most certainly, human is in loss,

3. Except those who believe and do good, righteous deeds, and exhort one another to truth, and exhort one another to steadfast patience.

Surah al-Asr was revealed in Mecca and comprises of three verses.

This surah is not only short and concise, but it is also a compilation which summarizes all the advice and warnings of the past surahs. In the surah, it emphasizes that all of the people are in a state of detriment and that faith is the only means of salvation and happiness. It was reported that Imam Shafi said: "If Allah had revealed this surah alone, even this short surah would have been sufficient for the guidance and success of mankind in life. It summarizes what the Qur'an taught."

Commentary

1. وَالْعَصْرِ *"By time,"*

The word "asr" is commonly used to define unrestricted time, and in particular the present time or an "era" (a time span of eighty or a hundred years). Initially, the commentators of the Qur'an emphasized that the meaning of "asr" is the Afternoon Prayer, the time of the Late Afternoon Prayer, a long duration of time and period, but in particular is the era of Prophet Muhammad, peace and blessings be upon him, or in other words the time when the Prophet was sent, and the period until the Last Day.

This means that "asr" is a collective word which has various meanings, and in view that there is no clear indication of the specific meaning, and that each of these meanings could be correct, it would be more appropriate to attribute this generally to "everything called *asr* (time)."

Allah the Almighty invokes "duha" (the morning) and "asr" (late afternoon). "Duha" is the first part of the day, and "asr" is the part which leads to the end of the day. This indicates that the life of mankind is coming to an end. In the Qur'an, the periods are divided into three in terms of the history of mankind:

1. The first period, the time before the Torah was sent to Prophet Musa, in other words, the period that ended with the destruction of the Pharaoh,

2. The middle period, the time from when the revelations of the Torah began until the coming of the Last Prophet,

3. The last period that began with the coming of Prophet Muhammad, peace and blessings be upon him, and will end with the Last Day, in other words as this means the era of the noble Prophet and his followers, when we say "asr," it should be recognized as this particular period.

This is the conclusion of the different approach of the commentators: O Muhammad! By the time (period) which in every aspect will be the scene for many great events, whether this is oppression, or in terms of productiveness a summary of the past eras, the final era, in other words your era, the period leading to the Last Day;

2. إِنَّ الْإِنْسَانَ لَفِي خُسْرٍ *"Most certainly, human is in loss."*

Every person, all races of mankind, the nations, the people of all periods and in particular those of the last period, with the exception of those defined in the Qur'an, are in a state of loss and destruction (al-Baqarah

2:55). Indeed, a human's capital is his life, whereas every breath, every hour of life is gradually fading, and with each breath is slowly approaching the end and the reckoning of the worldly favors. If those breaths belonged to the individual to do as he pleases and when he pleases, if the human was the owner of his own creation and structure, then that life would never end, and the individual would suffer no loss or harm if he consumed these breaths as he desired. But these breaths do not belong to humans, these breaths belong to the Creator the One who creates from nothing, therefore, this is an entrustment given to use and benefit from in the best way possible. The humans gain in life depends on the rewards of how he spent his life, and his dealings in this world.

3. إِلاَّ الَّذِينَ آمَنُوا وَعَمِلُوا الصَّالِحَاتِ وَتَوَاصَوْا بِالْحَقِّ وَتَوَاصَوْا بِالصَّبْرِ *"Except those who believe and do good, righteous deeds, and exhort one another to truth, and exhort one another to steadfast patience."*

Those attributed with these four qualities are not at a loss, but are those who gain:

1. Those who believe. These are the ones who acknowledge the unification of Allah, the Lord of the Universe and the Owner of the Day of Judgment, those who pledged to worship and obey Allah with all sincerity.

2. Those who do good, righteous deeds with their faith. In other words, those whose faith was not confined to their hearts, but rather performed these deeds according to their faith, to gain the pleasure of Allah believing that it was an act of righteousness; they continuously strived to do good, beneficial deeds for themselves, their families and friends, for their people and humanity, they performed the prescribed duties and avoided major sins and evil.

According to the Qur'an, deeds which are not based upon faith are not classified as righteous deeds. In the Qur'an, whenever it refers to righteous deeds it also mentions faith, and righteous deeds are mentioned after faith.

In the Qur'an, there is no mention of righteous deeds without faith. In addition, the Qur'an gives no prospect of reward for deeds performed without faith, even if these are good deeds. On the other hand, it is stated that sound and rewarding faith is the faith confirmed by good deeds. Because those of faith who do not perform good deeds, despite their claim of faith are in fact pursuing a path other than that prescribed by Allah and His Messenger.

Righteous duties are generally two kinds:

The first are the physical duties such as worship which are obligatory duties and beneficial to the individual. The other righteous duties are those which are beneficial to others such as alms and charity. The most important of these is the call to truth and striving on the path of truth. Thus, in addition to the aim of maturing faith and righteous deeds together with theoretic and practical powers; by striving for the perfection and salvation of both themselves and others, calling others to the truth of Allah and by jointly performing good deeds and reforming others, righteous deeds are commanded in particular by signifying these two aspects because they recognize the duty of agreeing in terms of endeavoring to help others to reach perfection, and cooperating on the path of truth.

3. And exhort one another to truth. In other words, their whole purpose and devotion is to Allah; their faith, deeds and words are all for the sake of Allah. By guarding the truth of everything, they encouraged one another to the truth of Allah, their every action is based on Allah's pleasure, they encouraged others to steadfastness and righteousness, unite in the truth, always called others to the truth of Allah, enjoined good and discouraged evil; in brief they advised and guided towards Allah and the truth, pledged to fulfill this and acted accordingly, their faith and actions were for the sake of Allah's truth and pleasure.

Every individual should bear the two attributes mentioned above. However, there are another two attributes to prevent loss and disappointment. After believing and performing righteous deeds, these are inspiring the truth and encouraging patience to one another. Firstly, this means those who believe and perform righteous deeds should not confine this to their own actions, but should also encourage societies of believers and righteousness. Secondly, every individual must acknowledge their own responsibility in guarding the society from corruption. This is why it is a religious duty of every member of the society to encourage the truth and patience to one another.

The word "truth" is the complete opposite of "false." Generally, this is used in two meanings: The first; is the statement of sincerity, justice and the truth. The second is exhorting the truth, a duty which is incumbent upon all humans. The meaning of exhorting the truth is a society of faith displaying the sensitivity of not standing by while others spread false knowledge and contradict the truth of Allah. Every individual in a society is not only obliged to personally enforce the truth, righteousness and justice in his own life, but at the same time must also advise others to fulfill this duty. This is the only means of guarding a community from moral decline and corruption. If there is no spirit in a community, then it is impossible for the society to avoid destruction and disappointment. Those who personally pursue the path of truth cannot remain on the true path if they stand by while the community becomes corrupted and will never escape destruction. This is why the Children of Israel were cursed by Prophet Dawud and Prophet Isa, peace be upon them, in Surah al-Maedah. The reason why they were cursed is because they did not restrain one another from evil acts which were widespread among the Jewish society during that period. (al-Maedah 5:78–79) Furthermore, in Surah al-A'raf it was revealed that the Children of Israel violated the prohibitions of the Sabbath (Saturday) and began to catch fish and due to this were inflicted with punishment, and only those who strived to prevent this sin escaped this punishment.

4. And exhort one another to steadfast patience.

In addition to exhorting the truth, for those of faith and their societies to avoid loss and destruction, the members of the society were conditioned to exhorting one another to patience. In other words, they should inspire patience to one another before all the difficulties, tribulations, hardships and deprivations for the sake of truth, and to guard the truth.

Although there is no denying that human nature has a great influence on the level of patience, an individual's upbringing, habits, determination, willpower and therefore faith also bears great significance. In these terms, just as patience is advised among the believers, they were also command-ed: *"O you who believe! Be patient; encourage each other to patience, vying in it with one another and outdoing all others in it; and observe your duties to Allah in solidarity, and keep from disobedience to Allah in due reverence for Him and piety, so that you may prosper!"* (Al Imran 3:200), because *"...Surely, Allah is with the persevering and patient"* (al-Baqarah 2:153), *"...Those who are patient will surely be given their reward without measure"* (az-Zumar 39:10). As related in the traditions "Patience is the key to contentment."[1] There are also famous phrases referring to patience "Patience is the companion of wisdom" and "Patience leads to salvation."

In view of this explanation and context, we clearly see that patience which is both praised and recommended is patience on the path of faith and righteous deeds, and the truth and goodness that is the sign of courage, loyalty and heroism. On the contrary, participating in all kinds of evil, succumbing to all kinds of contemptible acts, falling into enormity and whatever the consequences, not striving to escape; being caught up in falsehood and-no matter what- consenting to evil; such lowness which affirms idleness, humiliation and weakness cannot be classified as pure insensitivity. Consenting to evil acts is evilness and consenting to blasphemy cannot be classified as anything but disbelief.

Therefore, only those who bear the four attributes of faith, performing righteous deeds, exhorting the truth and patience are not at a loss, they are the exceptional ones. These four attributes are the sign of perfect faith. Clearly, those who have no faith will not reach salvation. However, this verse indicates that those who do not believe in Allah, perform righteous acts and exhort patience will not be exempt from some kind of loss. There-

---

[1] Daylami, *Firdaws*, 3/415; *Kashfu'l-Khafa*, I/27 (1590)

fore, the view of the Murji'ah sect that faith is complete without righteous deeds is not true. Indeed, as the Sunni sect states, there will be some kind of loss for the evildoers and the rebellious ones who believe but do not act according to their faith. As certainly rebellious believers will enter Hell although it may not be for eternity. Irrelevant whether their faith will eventually save them, the believers whose sins are greater than their good deeds will experience the torment of Hell until their sins are purified. May Allah save us all from the punishment of Hellfire!

SURAH AL-FIL

بِسْمِ اللهِ الرَّحْمٰنِ الرَّحِيمِ

أَلَمْ تَرَ كَيْفَ فَعَلَ رَبُّكَ بِأَصْحَابِ الْفِيلِ ۞ أَلَمْ يَجْعَلْ كَيْدَهُمْ فِي
تَضْلِيلٍ ۞ وَأَرْسَلَ عَلَيْهِمْ طَيْرًا أَبَابِيلَ ۞ تَرْمِيهِمْ بِحِجَارَةٍ مِنْ سِجِّيلٍ ۞
فَجَعَلَهُمْ كَعَصْفٍ مَأْكُولٍ ۞

Interpretation

In the Name of Allah, the All-Merciful, the All-Compassionate,

1. Have you considered how your Lord dealt with the people of the Elephant?
2. Did He not bring their evil scheme to nothing?
3. He sent down upon them flocks of birds.
4. Shooting them with bullet-like stones of baked clay;
5. And so He rendered them like a field of grain devoured and trampled.

This surah which was revealed in Mecca comprises of five verses. The surah takes its title form the first verse. It explains the story of the "ashab al-fil" or "The army of the elephant." When they wanted to destroy the Ka'ba, the house of Allah, the Almighty subjected them to their own evil scheme and protected His house from their rampage.

Commentary

1. أَلَمْ تَرَ كَيْفَ فَعَلَ رَبُّكَ بِأَصْحَابِ الْفِيلِ *"Have you considered (seen) how your Lord dealt with the people of the Elephant?"*

أَلَمْ تَرَ *"Have you considered?"* The addressee here is the Messenger of Allah. "Ru'yah" or "tara" (to see) can also mean the metaphor of vision, seeing with the heart, in other words O Muhammad! Certainly you know as if you witnessed it with your own eyes! Did news of this not reach you? However, according to certain interpreters of the Qur'an, although the addressee here appears to be the Prophet, it is in fact addressing the Qurayshi tribe, and at the same time, is also addressing all those who were in Saudi Arabia during that period.

كَيْفَ فَعَلَ رَبُّكَ *"How your Lord dealt?"* It is remarkable how the meaning here is the question "How," "Under what circumstances" rather than "ma fa'ala" *(*What He did). Indeed, this question is aimed at emphasizing the miraculous aspect of this event. Another astonishing, magnificent and wonderful aspect of this occurrence is its nature. In order to invoke the wonder of the act of Divinity, there was an emphasis placed on the essence of the event, for those blind to the detail of essence can never duly perceive the One of essence. This is why those incapable of deliberating the nature of this carefully, assume this to be an ordinary event and deceive themselves by believing they have perceived the truth. Indeed, in order to prevent such heedlessness and to display the amazingness of this act, Allah the Almighty particularly brings attention to the nature of the event by asking: *"Have you considered (seen) how your Lord dealt (with the people)?"*

بِأَصْحَابِ الْفِيلِ *"With the people of the elephant?"*

Here, Allah has not stated who the "ashab al-fil" are, where they came from, or why they came, as the addressees were familiar with the occurrences lead up to the event.

Ashab al-fil was the army of Abraha al-Ashram who had invaded the Yemen, and when he was the governor of Ethiopia, relying on his huge army and group of elephants lead by an elephant called Mahmud (mamud), Abraha marched towards the Ka'ba with this army destroying everything on their path in an attempt of demolishing the House of Allah. This is why they were called the "ashab al-fil" or the "army of the elephants" and among the Arabs, this year known as Amu al-Fil, the Year of the Elephant was the beginning of a new era. Prophet Muhammad, peace and blessings be upon him, was known to be born in the Year of the Elephant, and according to the most reliable reports, the noble Prophet was said to have been born fifty days after this event.

Certainly, this event was an indisputable miracle. There is no scientific explanation for the incident, and the account of the event is accurate as it occurred in Mecca forty years prior to the revelation of this surah, and many people of that period had personally witnessed this event. Despite the many adversaries, nobody objected to what the Prophet said.

This astonishing act of Divinity against Abraha's army is explained briefly in these four verses:

2. اَلَمْ يَجْعَلْ كَيْدَهُمْ فِي تَضْلِيلٍ *"Did He not bring their evil scheme to nothing?"*

Did He not overwhelm them amidst the ambush of their own deviance, conspiracies and traps? In other words, did Allah not inflict upon them suffering and cause them devastation? In Arabic, the words "kayd" and "makr" are used to define a secret plan to harm others. In the Turkish language, the word "kayd" also means to scheming, conspiring, plotting and ambush.

Because the verse "Did He not bring their evil scheme to nothing?" is a question aimed at evoking acknowledgment, it also means "Did you not see what Allah did?" So what were their plots, their schemes? As we know from reports, the army came with the elephants to destroy the Ka'ba to divert the people to perform the pilgrimage at the church Abraha constructed in Sana called Al-Quilays. They made several attempts both publically and in secret to achieve their objective, when they reached a place called Al-Mughammas a few miles away from Mecca, they were unsuccessful in prompting the elephant they called Mahmud into Mecca. Initially, this is what ruined their plan, then, as explained in the following verses, they were subjected to destruction like "asfin ma'kul" (devoured grain/crops). Therefore, not only were they unsuccessful in destroying the Ka'ba, but they were subjected to devastation, and their church was destroyed... was this not the case? Indeed, only Allah could prevent and reverse such a plot. This is what was inflicted by your Lord.

The word "kayd" is used in the verse, it means a "secret plot" to harm someone. Some may ask what the secrecy is here. It was no secret that Abraha who marched from the Yemen to Mecca with elephants and an army of sixty thousand men had come to destroy the Ka'ba. Therefore we cannot call this a secret plot. However, the secret objective of the Abyssinians was to defeat the Quraysh by demolishing the Ka'ba. They wanted to take control of the trade route stretching from Southern Arabia to Damascus and Egypt by intimidating the Arabs, but they concealed this. On the surface, their attack on the Ka'ba appeared to be in retaliation because the Arabs acted disrespectfully towards their church.

3. وَأَرْسَلَ عَلَيْهِمْ طَيْرًا أَبَابِيلَ **"He sent down upon them flocks of birds."**

In row upon row, flock upon flock, one after another, in scores from all directions.

"Tayr" is the plural for "tair" meaning flying birds. The word *tayran* portrays indecisiveness of the kind of bird, and suggests that these were unfamiliar, strange birds. Indeed, according to reports, these birds were groups of strange birds that were large, small, black, green and white.

Among other reports of the event, the birds came from the Yemen and from the ocean. This sudden attack from the flocks of strange birds appearing above like the dark clouds of a storm showered destruction upon them.

"Ababil" is a word for multiple. This means large groups or flocks that come one after the other. "Tayran ababil" means swarms, scores of birds coming one after another.

4. تَرْمِيهِمْ بِحِجَارَةٍ مِنْ سِجِّيلٍ **"Shooting them with bullet-like stones of baked clay;"**

These birds casted hard stones of baked clay at the army of the elephants.

"Sijjil" means stones of baked clay resembling brick. Therefore, this means stones made of clay and hardened by baking.

According to reports, these stones were the size of lentils, chickpeas and sheep droppings. Each bird carried three stones, one in each foot and one in the mouth, and it was reported that these stones entered through the skulls of the army, and exited leaving the body full of holes and infected wounds. Therefore, it would not be that difficult to imagine the condition of those subjected to the showering of stones thrown by flocks of birds from above, like machine guns firing bullets down upon them. This was the result:

5. فَجَعَلَهُمْ كَعَصْفٍ مَأْكُولٍ *"And so He rendered them like a field of grain devoured and trampled."*

Immediately they (the army of the elephants) were rendered like devoured grain by the Lord. Stating that "asf" is grain leaves, interpreters of the Qur'an gave a few examples:

1. The remains of the grain leaves left behind on the field after harvesting, which are blown by the wind and eaten by animals.
2. Broken straw scattered in the wind.
3. The grain leaves that fell to the ground and are eaten by the worms and insects, and these leaves are full of holes. This signifies that the bodies of Abraha and his army were riddled with holes.

"Ma'kul" means that what is eaten or has been eaten. Indeed, Allah rendered the army of the elephants like a field of "eaten grain leaves and straw" in such an astonishing way, and in such a short time. An invasive army which could not consider a force, a power that could possibly resist, which relying on its elephants and vast numbers assumed it could destroy the Ka'ba was suddenly defeated by a disaster of Divinity, and fell to the ground like a eaten up, devoured leaves and perished. Undoubtedly, if He wills, Allah the Almighty has the power to inflict punishments and tribulations to the rebellious ones that nobody could ever imagine!

And following the command "...*and keep My House pure for those who will go round it in devotion, and those who will stand in Prayer before it, and those who will bow down and prostrate themselves in worship*" (al-Hajj 22:26), in order to awaken the people to the fact that this was a Divine act particularly in preparation for the birth of Prophet Muhammad, peace and blessings be upon him, who was to come into this world to declare and promote unification in purifying the House of Allah, the surah begins with the words "Have you considered how your Lord dealt with them?" rather than "How the Lord dealt with them." Thus, this surah is an offering to the Prophet, tidings for the believers, a threat to the disbelievers and in particular rebuking the Quraysh who were heedless to the true value of this blessing.

SURAH AL-QURAYSH

بِسْمِ اللهِ الرَّحْمٰنِ الرَّحِيم

لِإِيلَافِ قُرَيْشٍ ۞ إِيلَافِهِمْ رِحْلَةَ الشِّتَاءِ وَالصَّيْفِ ۞ فَلْيَعْبُدُوا رَبَّ

هَذَا الْبَيْتِ ۞ الَّذِي أَطْعَمَهُمْ مِنْ جُوعٍ وَآمَنَهُمْ مِنْ خَوْفٍ ۞

Interpretation

In the Name of Allah, Most Gracious, Most Merciful

1. For favor of concord and security to the Quraysh,
2. Their concord and security in their winter and summer journeys,
3. Let them worship the Lord of this House,
4. Who has provided them with food against hunger, and made them safe from fear.

Surah al-Quraysh is also known as "Li-ilafi Quraysh." This surah was revealed in Mecca and comprises of four verses. The surah was given this title because it mentions the Quraysh in the first verse. It is closely related to the topic of the previous Surah al-Fil, and is virtually a continuation of this surah. It reveals the blessings granted to the Quraysh for protecting the Ka'ba.

The Reason for Its Revelation

When we take into consideration the favor of Allah regarding what happened in Mecca and the Ka'ba due to the attempted attack by the army of the elephants, although they should have been the first to accept the Prophet's call to the unification of Allah, the Quraysh persisted in polytheism, and their attempts of defiance and resistance was the reason for the revelation of this surah.

Commentary

1. لِإِيلَافِ قُرَيْشٍ *"For favor of concord and security to the Quraysh."*

"Ilaf" means accustomedness and familiarity. Because Allah granted the Quraysh ease in their trade expeditions to the Yemen during the winter, and Syria in the summer months to which they had become accustomed, it was their duty to worship Him.

According to some interpreters of the Qur'an, the meaning of "Li ilafi Quraysh" is to express amazement. In other words, when they were spread throughout the region, Allah gathered them together, and by securing the trade expeditions as a custom in their lives, He deemed this their means of wealth. But now they were ignoring their duty of worshipping Allah.

Whereas, leave the innumerous blessings granted to the Quraysh, being able to perform the trade expeditions safely by the favor of Allah alone was a huge blessing, so even for the sake of this alone it was their duty to worship and display gratitude to the Creator.

2. إِيلَافِهِمْ رِحْلَةَ الشِّتَاءِ وَالصَّيْفِ *"Their concord and security in their winter and summer journeys."*

Allah accustomed them to the winter and summer journeys (travelling to the Yemen in the winter and Damascus in the summer).

"Rihlat" means journey, expedition. The Quraysh would travel to the Yemen to trade in the winter and to Basra and Damascus during the summer. Likewise, they would also migrate to Taif during the summer months for trade or other reasons, and to Mecca in the winter. Even if the Quraysh were incapable of displaying gratitude and respect to Allah for the other blessings, they should at least gratify Him for the favor of this custom thus:

3. فَلْيَعْبُدُوا رَبَّ هَذَا الْبَيْتِ *"Let them worship the Lord of this House."*

In other words, so they abstain from rejecting the noble Prophet's call to faith and acknowledge the truth, abandon polytheism and rebelliousness, and worship the Lord of the Bayt al-Atiq (the Ancient House) that was protected by Allah from the army of the elephants, and perform worship and servitude in accordance with His command. Servitude and worship is performed facing towards the Ka'ba, not to the actual structure, but to the Lord of that sacred house. Unfortunately, some believers show more respect and regard to the structure of the Ka'ba than they show to its Lord, the Prophet and the Qur'an.

4. الَّذِي أَطْعَمَهُمْ مِنْ جُوعٍ وَآمَنَهُمْ مِنْ خَوْفٍ *"Who has provided them with food against hunger, and made them safe from fear."*

This is the fear dispelled by the army of the elephants. In addition, as revealed in the Qur'an *"Do they not consider that We have established (Mecca) a secure sanctuary while people are ravaged all around them?"* (al-Ankabut 29:67) while they lived amidst violence and evil, the Quraysh not only found security in the in the city of Mecca which surrounded the Ka'ba, but also travelled safely on their frequent trade expeditions which was the result of the supplication of their grandfather, Prophet Ibrahim, peace be upon him. He supplicated *"My Lord! Make this a land of security"* (al-Baqarah 2:126). Again, he prayed, *"…and provide them with the produce of the earth"* (Ibrahim 14:37). Therefore, was it not the duty of the Quraysh to worship the Lord who granted them sustenance and security?

Indeed, the Lord saved you (the Quraysh) from fearing safety which nobody was ensured in Arabia. During that period, the people were not able to sleep in safety anywhere in Arabia. They lived in constant fear and under threat of attack. Nobody had the courage to leave the boundaries of their own tribes, because when a person went out alone, it was virtually impossible for them to return safely, they were either killed or captured and subjected to slavery. No caravan was safe, as they were continuously exposed to being ambushed on the journey, their possessions could be seized at any time. Giving bribes to the leaders of the tribes on the route was the only means of continuing the journey in safety. However, the Quraysh of Mecca were totally secure from any danger. There was no threat of them being attacked, and there was no fear or danger of the enemy invading

Mecca. The Quraysh travelled throughout the land in large or small groups freely. Due to the Quraysh's title of being the keepers of the Ka'ba, nobody would attempt to harm or dare to challenge them. In fact, if one of the Quraysh were attacked while travelling alone, saying "I am a keeper of the Ka'ba" or "I am from Allah's sanctuary" was sufficient in securing their safety. Upon hearing this, the assailant would end the attack immediately. Because the tribes that lived on the Arabian Peninsula not only respected the House of Allah, but also the Meccans who lived in its vicinity: they referred to them as "The neighbors of the House of Allah, the habitants of Allah's sanctuary, the keepers of the Ka'ba and the people of Allah."

So the leaders of a society who earn the respect of the Arabs living both within and outside the Hijaz region opposed the Prophet because they believed that his call to faith and unification would damage their own interests, and could possibly be a threat to them personally. In this surah, it commands them not to defy unification this call conveys, but to accept this call and worship the Lord of the Ka'ba who bestows these blessings.

SURAH AL-MA'UN

بِسْمِ اللهِ الرَّحْمٰنِ الرَّحِيمِ

أَرَأَيْتَ الَّذِي يُكَذِّبُ بِالدِّينِ ۞ فَذَلِكَ الَّذِي يَدُعُّ الْيَتِيمَ ۞ وَلاَ يَحُضُّ

عَلَى طَعَامِ الْمِسْكِينِ ۞ فَوَيْلٌ لِلْمُصَلِّينَ ۞ اَلَّذِينَ هُمْ عَنْ صَلاَتِهِمْ

سَاهُونَ ۞ اَلَّذِينَ هُمْ يُرَاءُونَ وَيَمْنَعُونَ الْمَاعُونَ ۞

Interpretation

In the Name of Allah, the All-Merciful, the All-Compassionate,

1. Have you considered one who denies the Last Judgment?
2. That is he who repels the orphan,
3. And does not urge the feeding of the destitute.
4. And woe to those worshippers,
5. Those who are unmindful in their Prayers,
6. Those who want to be seen and noted,
7. Yet deny all assistance.

This surah consists of seven verses. According to some interpreters of the Qur'an, the first three verses were revealed in Mecca, and the other four verses in Medina. According to Mawdudi, this surah is Medinan (revealed in Medina): "In our opinion there is an internal piece of evidence in the surah itself which points to its being a Medani Revelation. It holds out a threat of destruction to those praying ones who are unmindful of their Prayers and who pray only to be seen. This kind of hypocrites were found only at Medina, for it was there that Islam and the Muslims gained such strength that Islam and the Muslims gained such strength that many people were compelled to believe from expedience, had to visit the Mosque, join the congregational Prayer and prayed only to be seen by others, so as to be counted among Muslims. Contrary to this is, in Mecca conditions were altogether different. No one had to pray to be seen. There it was difficult even for the believers to pray in congregation; they prayed secretly and if a person prayed openly he did so only at the risk of his life."

The title which means "Acts of kindness" comes from the last verse and general topic of the surah. It emphasizes that belief is the basis of the reward for the deeds and the acts performed for religion granted in the Hereafter, and that solidarity and kindness in the society is essential.

In brief, the surah mentions two groups of people, these groups are:

1. The ungrateful ones who deny the favors of Allah, and the disbelievers who deny the Day of Reckoning and Punishment.
2. The hypocrites who perform deeds and worship not for the sake of Allah, but for ostentation.

Commentary

1. أَرَأَيْتَ الَّذِي يُكَذِّبُ بِالدِّينِ *"Have you considered one who denies the Last Judgment?"*

Ara'ayta, meaning *"Have you considered (seen)?"* Initially, the addressee appears to be the Messenger of Allah. However, in accordance with the style of the Qur'an, in such circumstances is in fact addressing every individual of intelligence, in other words is generally addressing all those who are capable of perceiving the truth. The question here is intended to prompt astonishment. It is aimed at attracting attention to the words that follow. "Have you considered" means to witness, to see, as the points that follow are factors that every individual of perception is capable of seeing. This can also mean to understand, to acknowledge or contemplate. For example, we say "see!" and the meaning of this is to reflect, to consider. So if we perceive the word in these terms, the meaning of the verse could be "Consider the state of that person! He denies that he will be punished or rewarded for his actions."

The Reason for Its Revelation

According to reports; Abu Jahl was the guardian of an orphan. One day the young boy came to Abu Jahl virtually naked and asked for something from his own wealth (inherited from his father). Abu Jahl pushed him away and ignored his request. One of the Qurayshi leaders told the boy mockingly: "Go to Muhammad and complain so he will intercede for you." Because the young boy was unaware of their intention, he went to the Messenger of Allah and asked for his help. The Prophet would never reject the depraved, so together they went to Abu Jahl. Abu Jahl greeted and welcomed him, and after listening to the Prophet, Abu Jahl returned the orphans wealth. On witnessing this, the Quraysh began to taunt Abu Jahl saying "you too have abandoned your faith and accepted the religion of Muhammad." He replied "No! I have not abandoned my faith, but I saw two warriors holding spears, one on his left and one on his right, and I was afraid that they would kill me if I rejected his demand."

According to a narration by Ibn Abbas, this surah was reported to have been sent regarding a man who was both greedy and a hypocrite. In which case, this surah was revealed either due to one of these, or for similar reasons. However, this judgment was not aimed at them in particular, but generally to all such people.

The word "din" in this verse is used to define the Qur'anic guidance, the reward or punishment in the Hereafter for deeds and sins, and is also used to define the Islamic faith. But the first meaning appears to be more appropriate, as anyone who believes in the Hereafter could not possibly act in this way towards an orphan. Obviously, a person who ill-treats an orphan or abstains from feeding the poor does not believe in the Hereafter or fear Allah's warnings.

2. فَذَلِكَ الَّذِي يَدُعُّ الْيَتِيمَ *"That is he who repels the orphan."*

In other words, if you consider this you are heedful, if not then you should take this into consideration! Indeed, because they do not believe in religion or the punishment of the Hereafter, and because they do not fear Allah and regard orphans as being weak and vulnerable, these disbelievers repel, abuse, oppress and banish the orphans.

3. وَلاَ يَحُضُّ عَلَى طَعَامِ الْمِسْكِينِ "**And does not urge the feeding of the destitute.**"

And does not urge or encourage the feeding of the poor and helpless. He not only abstains from feeding the destitute, but does not encourage or advise his family or friends who have both the time and the means to care for those in need, or consider the helpless, whereas that sustenance belongs to the poor, not to the one who provides. This sustenance is the right of the orphans, and giving is the duty of those capable of providing. This is not a gift from the provider, on the contrary, he gives because it is an incumbent duty and the right of the orphans, which is the meaning of the verse: "*And in their wealth, the poor and the destitute had due share*" (adh-Dhariyat 51:19). This means taunting the poor and deprived is forbidden. Briefly, the one who feeds the poor is, in a sense, paying his debt.

While it is an Islamic duty for those who feel the necessity of living as a society in harmony and peace, who escaped poverty and exceeded fear and attained security with the help of Allah to worship Him and display gratitude and servitude; and in order to fulfill servitude, it is a duty to care for the orphans and the destitute, as certainly those who abstain from doing so when they possess the means will be punished; those who act to the contrary, who ill-treat and are unjust to orphans, who are ruthless and so uncompassionate that they refrain from providing the poor with the most vital necessity, sustenance are deviating from the debt of humanity, a despicable act for which a person must repent, ruthlessness such as ill-treating orphans and not caring for the poor was a practice of those who claimed that religion was a fabrication. However much it may be astonishing that a person does not believe in the Islamic faith, it is not really surprising that they can become accustomed to bad habits. The most astonishing point is the negligence of those who appear to be religious towards their physical and material duties; that they can be so miserly to the extent that they will even avoid giving a small amount of their wealth to the needy. Here, while "it'am'il-miskin" (urge the feeding of the poor) would be more general, the words "ta'am'il-miskin" is more subtle. Indeed, if the words used were "it'am'il-miskin," then the meaning would have been "he does not urge (others) to feed the poor," whereas the meaning of the words used, "Ta'am'il-miskin" means "He does not urge (others) to give away the food of the poor."

4. فَوَيْلٌ لِلْمُصَلِّينَ *"And woe to those worshippers."*

Or "shame upon those worshippers." In other words, shame on those who worship but will fall into the valley in Hell called "wayl," or to be more precise, shame on those who "appear" to believe and worship.

5. اَلَّذِينَ هُمْ عَنْ صَلَاتِهِمْ سَاهُونَ *"Those who are unmindful of their Prayers. (Those heedless to the importance of worship, who do not pay the necessary attention to Prayer)."*

They are unmindful, heedless of the Prayer. It is important to point out here that they are being reprimanded not for inattentiveness during the Prayer, but for their negligence of performing the Prayer. As forgetting or making a mistake during Prayer is not totally avoidable as every human can make mistakes. This is why Ata ibn Dinar said: All praise be to Allah, the One who said "Those who are unmindful of the Prayer" and not "Those who are unmindful in Prayer."

There are many explanations by interpreters of the Qur'an regarding the meaning of being "unmindful of the Prayers": Ignorance towards the significance of Prayers and not performing the Prayers as an important duty, neglecting the Prayers, paying no attention to the times of Prayers, praying after the prescribed time, not giving importance to being late for the Prayer, not regretting abandoning Prayer; and when the Prayer is performed, this is not with a pure intention and for the sake of Allah, performing worship for certain worldly benefits, praying in a hypocritical manner, praying in the presence of others, but abstaining from praying while alone, and performing the Prayers not with the devoutness of standing before Allah or the awareness of servitude, but for ostentation are all included in this meaning.

Two reports narrated by Ibn Jarir were cited as evidence regarding this topic.

One of which was narrated by Sa'd ibn Abi Waqqas, who said: I asked the Prophet the meaning of "The worshippers who are neglectful of their Prayer." He replied: "They are the ones who delay their Prayers."[2]

Another was reported by Abu Barzah al-Aslami, he said: When the verse "Those who are unmindful of their Prayers" was revealed, the Messenger of Allah said: "This is better for you than the world and what it contains. These are the ones who, when they pray, they expect no benevolence, and if they abandon the Prayer, they do not fear their Lord."[3]

It is important to emphasize here that distraction and deviation of thought during Prayer, not paying attention to the Prayers or continuously thinking about other things during the Prayer are two totally different aspects. The first is due to human weakness. Certain thoughts may enter the mind involuntarily. As soon as the believer realizes his attention has begun to deviate from the Prayer, he tries to refocus his attention on the Prayer. However, the second is classified as being negligent of the Prayer, as the Prayer of such a person is nothing more than physical movement because he bears no intention of worshipping or coming close to Allah, and does not believe in the religious duty or the importance of Prayer. His heart does not incline towards Allah even for a moment throughout the entire Prayer. Prayers of such a person end with the intention and emotions in which it began.

This also includes those who take pride in performing a few Prayers, who deceive themselves into believing this is what religion is, and abstain from fulfilling their duties of worship and servitude.

6. ٱلَّذِينَ هُمْ يُرَاءُونَ *"Those who want to be seen and noted."*

Whatever act they do is not performed for the sake of Allah, but for ostentation and in public where everyone can see.

---

2   *Sahih Muslim*, Masajid, 195; Bayhaqi, *As-Sunanu'l-Kubra*, 2/214
3   Suyuti, *Ad-Durru'l-Mansur*, 8/642

Although a majority of the scholars say these verses were revealed regarding the hypocrites, some also claim the surah was revealed regarding the disbelievers of Mecca.

According to this, it is clear that the polytheists worshipped, that they gave no importance to Prayer, were negligent towards the Prayer; that they worshipped not in a state of tranquility, but in heedlessness and negligence, and as a pastime, a form of entertainment. The verse *"Their Prayer at the House (in the Sacred Mosque) is nothing but whistling and hand-clapping…"* (al-Anfal 8:35), states that they prayed by clapping their hands and whistling and literally turned Prayer into a form of entertainment.

Prayer, giving charity, hajj and fasting are not forms of worship that emerged with the coming of Islam, but existed in the Divine religions in the past. In fact, it states that while he was still a baby in his crib, Isa (Jesus) told those around him: *"He has enjoined upon me the Prayer and the Prescribed Purifying Alms for as long as I live"* (Maryam 19:31). In the fifty fifth verse of the same surah, it reveals that Ismail (Ishmael) commanded his people to pray and give in charity. In the Qur'an, it repeatedly emphasizes that all of the Prophets preached the same principles; servitude to Allah, righteousness and belief in the Hereafter to their people.

7. وَيَمْنَعُونَ الْمَاعُونَ *"Yet deny all assistance."*

"Ma'un": According to the dictionary definition and interpretations of the Qur'an, this is the name given to charity, favors and benevolence, anything of little benefit or value; a plate, jug, pot, bowl, spade or other housewares that neighbors borrow to one another, or equipment that may contribute to the needs of others.

In which case, the meaning of this verse is as follows; they avoid giving anything, even the most trivial of aid such as sustenance, indeed they can be so greedy, so miserly. It is evident that these individuals abstain from giving charity.

The behavior of such individuals who pray in this manner, who appear to be religious but neglect Prayers, who perform obligatory duties to appear pious but abstain from providing charity—even though they are not rejecting faith like the disbelievers—who reproaching the orphans and refrain from giving charity to the poor and destitute is quite astonishing, as performing righteous deeds is one of the principles of faith, and as we said earlier both faith and righteous deeds are mentioned together in the Qur'an. Although there are some individuals who claim to be religious and appear to fulfill the duties of worship, they are only deceiving themselves by presuming that they have in fact fulfilled all of the religious duties made incumbent upon them. Such people take pleasure in asking for the sake of Allah, but avoid giving the most trivial thing for the sake of Allah, avoid helping the servants of Allah, and although they have the means, avoid the expenditure necessary in fulfilling the commands of Allah.

As a result, the main factor which prevents people from committing evil, which encourages kindness and induces the sense of compassion, is beyond doubt belief in the Hereafter. Those who do not believe in the world beyond have no consideration for the orphans, the deprived or the weak. It is extremely uncommon for such people to consider anyone but themselves. This is why this surah reveals that those who do not believe in the Hereafter, are heedless in their Prayers and do not give any importance to the spirit of worship do not consider others, they perform righteous acts for show, are not sincere and do not provided help to others.

Therefore, those who believe in the reckoning and punishment of the Hereafter are compassionate towards orphans; help the poor, perform the Prayers with sincerity and devotion, with reverence and tranquility, punctually and consistently. They abhor ostentation, worship with devotion, not for show, and are always ready to help others.

SURAH AL-KAWTHAR

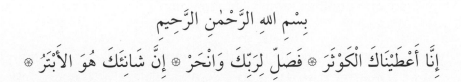

بِسْمِ اللهِ الرَّحْمٰنِ الرَّحِيم

إِنَّا أَعْطَيْنَاكَ الْكَوْثَرَ ۞ فَصَلِّ لِرَبِّكَ وَانْحَرْ ۞ إِنَّ شَانِئَكَ هُوَ الْأَبْتَرُ ۞

Interpretation

In the Name of Allah, the All-Merciful, the All-Compassionate,

1. We have surely granted you (unceasing) abundant good.
2. So pray to your Lord, and sacrifice.
3. Surely it is the one who offends you who is cut off.

This surah revealed in Mecca is one of the surahs sent during the early days of the revelations. It consists of three verses, is the shortest surah of the Qur'an, affirms the abundance and prosperity Allah bestowed upon His Messenger and His sovereignty over the hearts of humanity.

The Reason for Its Revelation

According to reports regarding this subject, there is agreement that this surah was revealed because the Prophet was called "abtar," or a man with no linage (sons) by some of his enemies who abhorred him due to his faith. But who called him this? And why did they call him this? There are various reports conveying the reasons. According to a majority, As ibn Wail said "I am an enemy of Muhammad, and the enemy of people is cut off." While according to some, Uqba ibn Abu Mu'ayt said that the Prophet was cut of (linage) because he had no sons.

It was reported by Ibn Abbas: The Prophet's eldest child was Qasim, followed by Zaynab, Abdullah, Umm Kulthum, Fatima and then Ruqayyah. Qasim died in Mecca, he was the first child of the Prophet to die, and then Abdullah died. Following the death of Abdullah, As ibn Wail as-Sahmi said Muhammad's linage has come to an end. Allah the Almighty sent the verse *"Surely it is the one who offends you who is cut off."*

Some say that after the death of the Prophet's son Ibrahim, the polytheists visited one another saying "Muhammad's linage came to an end tonight."

Indeed, among the reports regarding the reason for its revelation the only report signifying that this was a Medinan surah was the report regarding the death of Ibrahim. All other reports indicate that this is Meccan which appears to be the most popular view.

According to these reports, it is quite evident that when the disbelievers said *abtar*, they were in fact implying "the end of linage." By saying this, they were actually exposing their hostility and rejoicing that the mission of the Prophet had come to an end. These words must have grieved the Prophet immensely, as he is informed that due to Prophethood, he was granted abundance, that his name would be remembered, that they are the ones who will be "cut off," and he was commanded to pray to Allah alone for the greatest of all favors bestowed, his Prophethood, and sacrifice for the sake of Allah.

This excellent surah, with its conciseness, subtle points and signs is virtually a follow up of the previous surahs, and a basis for the next surah. In particular, its relationship with Surah al-Ma'un is that it is rather like a response. Especially the relation in response to denial, an attribute of disbelievers and hypocrites; justification in response to ruthlessness and miserliness; benevolence and kindness in response to deviating in worship; being steadfast in Prayer in response of ostentation, devotion and sincerity "for your Lord"; in response of rejecting small kindnesses, sacrifice and feeding the poor and destitute are well worth reflecting upon.

Commentary

1. إِنَّا أَعْطَيْنَاكَ الْكَوْثَرَ *"We have surely granted you (unceasing) abundant good."*

The addressee here is the Messenger of Allah. The words "We granted" denotes honor. When Allah said, "We granted" rather than "We will grant," He used the past tense form stating that this had already been granted, as indeed this promise will certainly be fulfilled. So the past tense form was used to place more emphasis on the subject, as if the event had already occurred.

"Al-Kawthar," which linguistically means abundance, defines unlimited abundance, a plentitude of such greatness, the word derives from "kathrat" meaning a lot. Additionally, this is also the name of a river in Paradise from which all the streams in Paradise flow. According to some, this is used to describe "khayr al-kathir," or the abundance, the plentitude of good which also includes aspects such as the Prophethood, the Qur'an, the position of intercession and knowledge.

However, with reference as to whether this bears a particular meaning in religious language or not, there are various explanations presented by scholars of the Qur'an, in total around twenty six opinions. Here a few of the most popular views:

The first: The most common view in a majority of the commentaries of the successors and early scholars, is that Kawthar is the name of a river in Paradise. This was also authenticated in reports by the Prophet: "Kawthar is a river which my Lord has granted me in Paradise."[4] In some reports, Kawthar is a pool bearing the abundance of good. The righteous of my followers will drink from it on the Day of Judgment; its jugs are equal in numbers to the stars in the sky. Some from among them will be pulled away, whereupon I will say "O Lord! My followers!" Then Allah will say "You do not know what they did after you." And according to these traditions of the Prophet, in clarifying the meaning of the term "abundance of good," he is specifically

---

[4] *Sahih Muslim*, Salah, 53–54

declaring that this is a river or pool in Paradise. Regarding the description of this river, Imam Ahmad ibn Hanbal, Bukhari, Muslim, Ibn Majah, Nasa'i, Ibn Jarir and others narrated various reports by Anas, Aisha, Ibn Umar and Ibn Abbas stating characteristics such as "A river whose banks were of hollowed pearl, and whose scent is of musk, it is whiter than milk and sweeter then honey, its width and length is equal to the distance between the East and West, its depth covers a timespan of seventy thousand years, those who drink from it never experience thirst, those who perform ablutions from its water will never perish, those who violate my treaty or kill the people of my house are forbidden from drinking from it."

It mentions in Islamic books that because the traditions about the fountain or river of the Prophet are agreed upon by majority, for Sunni Muslims it is an incumbent duty to believe in this. In accordance with this surah, although there is no doubt that believing the Kawthar was granted to the Messenger of Allah is a duty on all Muslims, while believing it to be either a river or pool may be correct, believing it to be one or the other cannot be classified a duty. Indeed, there are other opinions. Namely:

The second: According to a report by Ikrima, it is the honor of Prophethood. As Prophethood is a universal leadership for good in both worlds necessary for the prosperity in religion and in the world, an abundance of good (*khayr al-kathir*) which is a Divine favor, and as a result is a favor of mercy.

The third: That this is referring to the scholars of the Islamic community. Indeed, the scholars who in terms of knowledge and morals are the successors of the Prophets are certainly the means of guidance and prosperity.

The fourth: The Prophet's followers and society were of a majority. Allah the Almighty granted him such a prosperous community and Companions that it was pledged and tidings were given in the authentic traditions of the Prophet that more than half of the habitants of Paradise would be his followers.

The fifth: The Prophet had many followers and descendants. The Prophet being granted these tidings appears to be consistent in the denial of his enemy's immoral behavior of calling him "abtar" following the death of his son. In other words, O Muhammad! Your progeny will not end with the death of your sons as the enemy anticipated. In fact, on the contrary, this means we will grant you many, a great many generations that would never disappear, and that is exactly what happened.[5]

However, in addition to all of these explanations, a majority of scholars insisted on the meaning "abundance of good," as in terminology, this is the most comprehensive meaning. This can also include every "abundance of good" imaginable, and indeed, that which is unimaginable, reserved for both this world and the Hereafter.

Therefore, to pay gratitude for the benevolence of the Kawthar, as prescribed in the verse *"If you are thankful, I will most certainly give you more..."* (Ibrahim 14:7):

2. فَصَلِّ لِرَبِّكَ وَانْحَرْ *"So pray to your Lord, and sacrifice."*

Certainly, the benevolence of the Kawthar requires fulfilling these commands in the most excellent manner.

فَصَلِّ لِرَبِّكَ *"So pray to your Lord,"* which means, pray to your Lord alone with unification and piety. Therefore, the command "pray" was recorded to depict that Prayer must be performed with all these motives, stating the condition that it is "to your Lord."

وَانْحَرْ *"...and sacrifice."* In addition to performing Prayer, sacrifice contrarily to those who abstain from charity(who avoid giving even the smallest, most trivial things), forsake wealth and live assets (such as camels, cattle, and sheep and goats) and sacrifice in the Name of your Lord. As the command "sacrifice" was given after "pray," the words "to your Lord" are prevailing here. This means "pray to your Lord" and "sacrifice for your Lord," which is in fact commanding that these two acts of worship must be performed with a pure intention for the sake of Allah. As Prayer which is

---

[5] Yazır, Elmalılı Hamdi, *Kur'an-ı Kerim Tefsiri*, "Kevser Suresi"

not performed for the sake of Allah is not classified as worship, sacrifice which is not performed in the Name of Allah is not accepted as sacrifice. As the sacrifice of those who do not proclaim the Name of Allah, or mention a name other than Allah is "...offered in the name other than Allah..." and is not classified as sacrificed, and is therefore prohibited.

This verse bears the meaning of steadfastness in worship, and is also encouraging voluntary Prayers. Additionally, it emphasizes that this alone is insufficient, that in addition to physical worship such as Prayers, spiritual and material worship such as sacrifice is also a requirement of faith, and in accordance with the verse *"Say: 'My Prayer, and all my acts and forms of devotion and worship, and my living and my dying are for Allah alone, the Lord of the worlds. He has no partners; thus have I been commanded, and I am the first and foremost of the Muslims'"* (al-An'am 6:162–163) all forms of worship must be performed for the sake of Allah alone.

While believe the command "pray" in this verse as being the five Prescribed Prayers, others consider this to be the Prayer of Eid al-Adha (Festival of Sacrifice). According to some, this means to perform the Prayers of Eid followed by the sacrificing of an animal. However, when considering the context on a whole, the meaning is: "O Messenger of Allah! Your Lord has provided you with such abundance, He granted you such a great favor, so pray and sacrifice for His sake." When this command was given, not only the Qurashi or Arabian polytheists, but the polytheists throughout the entire world were worshipping, and sacrificing for their own man-made "gods." The purpose here, contrary to the polytheists, by praying and sacrificing for the sake of Allah alone, was to represent steadfastness on their own path.

In Medina, on the tenth day (*nahr*) of Dhi'l-Hijjah the Prayers of Eid al-Adha and the sacrifice were deemed lawful for the people. However, the practice of this Prayer and sacrifice was not established directly with this verse, but by the command and practices of the Prophet. "There are three things that have been made obligatory for me but not for you: Observing the Witr Prayer, the sacrifice (on Eid al-Adha) and performing the Duha (Midmorning) Prayer."[6] Therefore, there are things that although were obligatory upon the Prophet, were not obligatory on his followers. In which case the commands here: "Pray" and "sacrifice" are also commands as such. In addition the traditions warn us: "Whoever has the financial ability to offer a sacrifice but does not do so, he should not approach our place or Prayer,"[7] and "Perform the sacrifice, for it is the practice of your father Ibrahim."[8]

Therefore, performing the sacrifice after Eid Prayers became established by the practice and command of the Messenger of Allah. It was agreed upon that the sacrifice was a tradition, a Sunnah of the Prophet that he never abandoned. Whereas a tradition of such is walking on the path displaying the manifests of faith, and to the extent that it is virtually an obligatory act. Although traditions of this kind are not referred to as obligatory meaning an incumbent practice, according to the Hanafi school of jurisprudence, when there is indecisiveness regarding an obligation such as "He should not approach our place of Prayer," subjects bearing indefinite evidence are classified as Wajib (necessary) which is close to being an incumbent duty. This is why sacrifice is classified as Wajib in a clear report by Imam Abu Hanifa.

The kinds of animals prescribed for sacrifice revealed in Surah al-An'am described as being *"Eight in pairs"* (al-An'am 6:143) are sheep, goats, camels, cattle both male and female adults as defined in the Islamic law, and affirmed by the practice of Prophet Muhammad, peace and blessings be upon him.

Generally, Prayer and charity are mentioned together in the Qur'an, whereas in this verse there is no mention of charity, it says sacrifice, because the purpose of sacrifice is also classified as charity, a form of aid which is distributed to the poor. In which case, the purpose of this shortest surah of the Qur'an was in fact helping the poor.

In brief, what has been defined until this point is as follows: Because We granted you the "Kawthar," pray the Lord in gratitude for His favor to

---

6   Ahmad ibn Hanbal, *Musnad*, I/231; Suyuti, *Ad-Durru'l-Mansur*, I/536

7   *Sunan ibn Majah*, Adahi, 2; Ahmad ibn Hanbal, *Musnad*, 2/321

8   *Sunan ibn Majah*, Adahi, 3

you with piety, both physically and materially with every limb of your body, and in addition to the Prayer, offer sacrifice. If you devoutly worship Allah with piety and unification, and remember this blessing by performing good deeds, there is no likelihood of your Lord ceasing His favors to you.

3. إِنَّ شَانِئَكَ هُوَ الْأَبْتَرُ "*Surely it is the one who offends you who is cut off.*"

Surely, whoever resents, harbors hostility, hates or offends you, is the one who is cut off. He is the one whose linage will cease, who will be cut off from his descendants, who will be dishonored, not you O Muhammad! Your generations that come after you, the Companions and helpers, each of whom were like your own children and family, and your beloved followers will multiply immensely. Your religion, your Book, your beautiful name, your excellent reputation, prosperity and kindness will remain forever. You will attain favors in the Hereafter impossible to explain, favors that never cease. Undoubtedly, those who offend, who underestimate such abundance will remain unfaithful and worthless.

Although the actual meaning of the word "abtar" is cut off (progeny severed), this word is most commonly used as one whose tail is cut off. Due to the fact that the tail is on the back, there is no continuation, in other words those who have no offspring, no descendants, those who leave behind no trace, or that which has no prosperity was referred to as *abtar*.

"Any important affair that does not begin in the Name of Allah is *abtar*."[9] The meaning of the word "abtar" in this hadith is non-continuing, non-prosperous, deficient, remaining incomplete.

Those who hate and abused you by calling you *abtar* due to the death of your son are themselves *abtar* in every aspect. They are the ones who are truly deficient and incomplete. Certainly, the enemies of the Prophet never prospered. Either their progeny ceased in terms of materialism, or in spiritual terms their prosperity and existence became extinct, and as a re-

---

9   Bayhaqi, *As-Sunanu'l-Kubra*, 3/209

sult they perished amidst a life of misery and contempt. The offspring of those who bore a progeny were never prosperous.

Those insensitive individuals used the death of the Prophet's son as an excuse to call him *abtar*, whereas due to the fact that the children of the Prophet's daughters and the children of their children were of his linage, they were the successors, the children, grandchildren and descendants of the Prophet, his progeny never ceased. In addition, although the Prophet was the father of several sons, there is certainly wisdom in the fact that none of them lived for a long period, and that his progeny continued through his daughters alone. This was described as him being the last of the Prophets. He was granted both male and female offspring to clarify the abundance and perfection of his carnal power in addition to his spiritual power, however, due to the fact that the chain of Prophethood was sealed with Prophet Muhammad, peace and blessings be upon him, his religion and Book would remain until the Last Day, and if his sons had survived, them being honored with Prophethood would not be in accordance with this, as surviving and not being granted the honor of Prophethood may have prevented them from being dutiful offspring, thus overshadowing their honor, therefore the death of his sons in infancy (in a state of innocence) may have been more favorable both for them and for Allah's Messenger.

If the Prophet's sons had survived him, although they would not have been granted Prophethood, it would have been in accord for them to be rendered successors of the imamate, but because the imamate successorship would have been confined to the descendants of the Prophet rather than competency, this restriction would have appeared to be inconsistent with the Prophethood of Muhammad, peace and blessings be upon him, in general. As there was no probability of the Prophethood or imamate of women, it was impossible for his daughters to be his successors. Therefore, the logical meaning and wisdom in the continuation of the Prophet's progeny through his daughters, and the early death of his sons can be summarized by these two reasons: Because there was to be no Prophethood after him, and so the imamate and leadership would not be bound to ancestry alone. On the contrary, it was certainly not as the Arabs of the Period of Ignorance assumed, that following the death of his sons, the Prophet's progeny would end and the offspring of his daughters would not be classified as his progeny. Clearly, this last verse contains predictions regarding the future.

The disbelievers spoke like this in the anticipation that the Prophet's physical, and in particular his spiritual progeny would end. However, with the hundreds of thousands of followers, and the millions of Muslims who fill the mosques throughout the entire world, and in particular the mosques in the two holy cities is a spectacular example of the Divine abundance mentioned in this surah.

SURAH AL-KAFIRUN

بِسْمِ اللهِ الرَّحْمٰنِ الرَّحِيمِ

قُلْ يَا أَيُّهَا الْكَافِرُونَ ۞ لاَ أَعْبُدُ مَا تَعْبُدُونَ ۞ وَلاَ أَنْتُمْ عَابِدُونَ مَا أَعْبُدُ ۞

وَلاَ أَنَا عَابِدٌ مَا عَبَدْتُمْ ۞ وَلاَ أَنْتُمْ عَابِدُونَ مَا أَعْبُدُ ۞ لَكُمْ دِينُكُمْ وَلِيَ دِينِ ۞

Interpretation

In the Name of Allah, the All-Merciful, the All-Compassionate,

1. Say "O you unbelievers!

2. I do not, nor ever will, worship that which you worship.

3. Nor are you those who ever worship what I worship.

4. Nor am I one who do ever worship that which you have ever worshipped.

5. And nor are you those who do and will ever worship what I ever worship.

6. You have your religion, and I have my religion."

This surah was revealed in Mecca. It consists of six verses and takes its name from the first verse. It commands that believers must display their determination in unification before the disbelievers, and that they should not force the disbelievers to accept the Islamic faith, but should rather leave it to their own choice. Thus, emphasizing the freedom of religion in Islam.

This surah is also known as the "Surah of Worship" or the "Surah of Sincerity." This is why surahs al-Kafirun and al-Ikhlas together are sometimes called "Ikhlasayn" (two surahs of sincerity).[10] Indeed, we see in traditions narrated by Ibn Umar and the Prophet's dear wife Aisha, that the Prophet recited Surah al-Kafirun and Surah al-Ikhlas in the two *rakats* (units) of Prayer before the obligatory Prayers of Fajr (Morning) Prayers, and in the two units of Prayer following the obligatory Prayers of Maghrib (Evening) Prayers, and that these two surahs were called the purity of faith.

Both Abu Ya'la and Tabarani reported the following tradition as an elevated narration:

"Shall I inform you of the word that will protect you from polytheism? Before you go to sleep, recite the Surah al-Kafirun."[11] In another tradition, the noble Prophet said: "Surah al-Kafirun is equivalent to one fourth of the Qur'an."[12]

Although many different explanations were given regarding this, the most simplest to understand is as follows: in one perspective, the meaning of Qur'an here can be defined briefly as: Worship, transactions, judgments of the Hereafter and the parables. As for this surah, the reason why it is equivalent to a fourth of the Qur'an is because its declaration of unification and sincerity, the spirit of worship, is mandatory.

The Reason for Its Revelation

Certain leaders of the Quraysh made a proposal to the Messenger of Allah, accept our religion, and we will accept yours, worship our gods for one year and we will worship your Lord for one year. The Prophet said: "I seek refuge in Allah from associating others with Him." Then they proposed, at least touch some of our gods, if you do this we will accept you and worship your Allah. Then this surah was revealed. The next morning, the Prophet went to the Sacred Mosque where a group of influential members of the Quraysh were sitting. The Prophet stood over them and recited this surah, and finally the Quraysh gave up hope of achieving their objective.[13]

---

[10]   *Sunan ibn Majah*, Iqama, 102

[11]   Suyuti, *Ad-Durru'l-Mansur*, 8/657

[12]   Qurtubi, 20/224; Alusi, *Ruhu'l-Ma'ani*, XV, 2/319

[13]   Suyuti, *Ad-Durru'l-Mansur*, 8/654

Initially, the addressees of this surah were the Quraysh, as indeed, the surah was revealed following these proposals from members of the Quraysh. However, this surah was by no means confined to that period or to those individuals alone. This directive conveyed in the Qur'an is valid for Muslims until the Day of Judgment. Irrelevant of the form, polytheism must be avoided both verbally and physically.

Commentary

1. قُلْ يَا أَيُّهَا الْكَافِرُونَ *"Say: 'O you unbelievers!'"*

Imam ar-Razi presented around forty possible reasons for this surah beginning with the call "Say," the detailed explanations are exceedingly long. The first and foremost being to emphasize that the Prophet was assigned by Allah, and these were the direct words of Allah. The Prophet was aware that when he referred to them as disbelievers saying "O you unbelievers," the Quraysh became angry with him. This is evidence that he was protected by Allah, and therefore paid no attention to the disbelievers or their false gods.

The call "O you unbelievers" was not addressing the disbelievers in general, but was particularly aimed at certain individuals who Allah knew would never accept faith. The word "unbelievers" was not aimed at insulting those who disbelieved, but rather to express a reality. In Arabic, the word "kafir" is use to define the rejecters, those who do not believe. The opposite of this is "mu'min" or believer, in other words, the one who acknowledges and submits. Allah commanding His Messenger to say "O unbelievers" actually means "O those who reject my Messengership and ignore the directives I conveyed." In the same way, the objective when using the word "mu'min" is "those who believe in Muhammad."

In the surah it says "O unbelievers" not "O polytheists." Therefore the addressees of this surah are not only the polytheists, it is everyone who does not believe that Muhammad is Allah's Messenger and denies that the order he conveyed was from Allah. These may be the Jews, Christians, Zoroastrians or the polytheists. The addressees of this call were neither the

Quraysh, nor the Arab disbelievers or polytheists of Arabia, but rather all the disbelievers and polytheists in the entire world.

Addressing the rejecters as "O unbelievers" is like referring to someone as "O enemies, O adversaries." In which case, when such an address is made, it is necessary to recognize who is being targeted by the adjective generally, not those who are addressed. Therefore, if the individual bears the attribute of being an "unbeliever," then he is an addressee of this surah. When a person abandons adversity and hostility, and embraces and safeguards his faith, then he is no longer an addressee of this surah.

Here, the words "O unbelievers" is not due to their individuality, but due to their disbelief. Those who persist in disbelief until death will be continue to be the addressees of this surah, whereas those who embrace faith are not.

2. لَا أَعْبُدُ مَا تَعْبُدُونَ *"I do not, nor ever will, worship that which you worship."*

In brief, I will never worship the idols you classify as Allah that you expect me to glorify. I never worshipped these idols in the past, and I never will.

3. وَلَا أَنْتُمْ عَابِدُونَ مَا أَعْبُدُ *"Nor are you those who ever worship what I worship."*

You never worshipped the Allah of truth that I worship with unification and sincerity, you never have in the past and never will. He is the One Allah, and I worship the Allah of truth. He is Allah, the Lord of the universe, whereas you worship idols and stone. How can there possibly be any comparison between worshipping the One of Compassion and pursuing desires and worshipping idols!

4. وَلَا أَنَا عَابِدٌ مَا عَبَدْتُمْ *"Nor am I one who do ever worship that which you have ever worshipped."*

This verse reiterates the rejection of worshipping idols mentioned previously, and leaves the disbelievers in a state of disappointment. He is virtually saying: I will not worship these idols not now or in the future. I will never worship what you worship for as long as I live.

5. وَلَا أَنْتُمْ عَابِدُونَ مَا أَعْبُدُ *"And nor are you those who do and will ever worship what I ever worship."*

6. لَكُمْ دِينُكُمْ وَلِيَ دِينِ *"You have your religion, and I have my religion."*

"You have your religion" in other words, you are the only one accountable for the responsibility, punishment and consequences of these actions. "And I have my religion." Islam, the religion of truth is my religion. Its rewards and favors belong to me. You are responsible for your acts of polytheism, and I am responsible for my faith in the unification of Allah. This clearly proves that the Prophet never practiced the worship of the disbelievers, and confirms that he worshipped the one Allah, the Almighty.

Interpreters of the Qur'an say: In the first two verses, it emphasized that people are totally different in the recognition of Allah. The polytheist's idols are their deities, and the noble Prophet's deity is Allah. In the last two verses, it states that they are totally different in their forms of worship. Virtually as if the Prophet is saying "Neither our deity nor our worship is the same." In other words, my religion and your religion are completely different. I am not one who will worship your idols and you do not worship the Allah I worship. I cannot worship your manmade Idols and you are not prepared to worship my Allah. Therefore our paths will never unite. This statement is not to appear tolerable to the disbelievers, but to declare that all relations between them will remain severed for as long as they persist in idol worshipping. At the same time, this also indicates that neither the Messenger of Allah nor his followers will ever compromise with the disbelievers regarding religion, and they should therefore abandon all hope of them doing so.

Indeed, this surah that was revealed in response to such suggestions from the polytheists, states that every individual has the right to their own opinion, is at liberty to act how they wish, and will be accountable for their own actions.

In fact, the Qur'an brought freedom of conscience and did not command that disbelievers should be forced into accepting the Islamic faith, but states that the Prophet is a guide, an advisor and conveyor rather than an enforcer of religion: "...*what rests with you is only to convey the Message fully and clearly.*" Many verses such as Al Imran 3:20; an-Nahl 16:82; ash-Shura 42:48 affirm that the duty of the Prophet is to convey the truth, not to force the people to accept the Islamic faith; and verses such as "...*you are not one to compel them...*" (Qaf 50:45) confirm that the Prophet is not an enforcer of compeller. The verses like: "There is no compulsion in religion" (al-Baqarah 2:256) and "*Say: 'O humankind! Assuredly there has come to you the truth from your Lord. Whoever, therefore, chooses the right way follows it but for his own good; and whoever chooses to go astray, goes astray but to his own harm. I am not one appointed as a guardian over you to assume responsibility for you'*" (Yunus 10:108) are the most explicit statements regarding the freedom of conscience.

In view of this verse (al-Kafirun 109:6), Imam Hanifa and Imam Shafi perceive disbelievers as one people irrelevant of the differences between each other's religions, and say that a Jew can inherit a Christian, and a Christian can inherit a Jew, or a disbeliever of one religion can inherit the disbeliever of another religion.

SURAH AN-NASR

بِسْمِ اللهِ الرَّحْمٰنِ الرَّحِيمِ

إِذَا جَاءَ نَصْرُ اللهِ وَالْفَتْحُ ۞ وَرَأَيْتَ النَّاسَ يَدْخُلُونَ فِي دِينِ اللهِ

أَفْوَاجًا ۞ فَسَبِّحْ بِحَمْدِ رَبِّكَ وَاسْتَغْفِرْهُ إِنَّهُ كَانَ تَوَّابًا ۞

Interpretation

In the Name of Allah, the All-Merciful, the All-Compassionate,

1. When Allah's help comes, and victory,

2. And you see people entering Allah's Religion in throngs,

3. Then glorify your Lord with His praise, and ask Him for forgiveness; for He surely is One Who returns repentance with liberal forgiveness and additional reward.

Surah an-Nasr was revealed during the Medinan period and consists of three verses.

In a narration from Bukhari, Aisha reported that following the revelation of the Surah an-Nasr, the Prophet frequently recited "O Lord! I glorify You with praise. O Lord! Forgive me" during the Prayer.[14]

Although he was still only very young, Umar would call Ibn Abbas to gatherings, and the elders of the Companions found this strange. One day at one of these gatherings, Umar asked the Companions "What do you say regarding the statement of Allah "When Allah's help comes and victory?" to which they gave various answers. Then Umar asked Ibn Abbas, he re-

---

[14] *Sahih al-Bukhari*, Tafsir as-Surah 110/1, 2; *Sahih Muslim*, Salah, 218–220

plied "That is the sign of the Prophet's death about which he had been informed." Umar replied "I do not know anything about it other than what you have said."[15]

Alusi said: In many reports by Ibn Abbas and others, that following the revelation of this surah, the Prophet said "My death has been announced."[16] This is why this verse is also referred to as the "farewell" surah.

In a narration by Bayhaqi: "When this surah was revealed, the Prophet called Fatima and said "My death has been announced." At first she wept, and then she smiled. When she was asked the reason for this, Fatima replied "When my father informed me of his death, I wept, then he told me that I would be the first of his household to meet him in Paradise, then I smiled." There are reports that this surah was revealed during the Farewell Pilgrimage in Mecca.

According to some interpreters of the Qur'an, this was the last complete surah of the Qur'an to be revealed.

Commentary

1. إِذَا جَاءَ نَصْرُ اللهِ وَالْفَتْحُ *"When Allah's help comes, and victory"*

"Nasrullah" means the help of Allah. The help pledged is that which would make the Prophet triumphant over the enemy, and victory. The meaning of this is the Prophet's victory over the Quraysh and the Arabs, and the conquest of Mecca. It was also said to be the help of Allah, and the command of the conquest of the provinces of polytheists. The objective of the word conquest is not restricted to the conquest of towns or regions, but is intended more at the conquest of faith and Islam in the hearts. This is the conquests incumbent following the conquest of Mecca, the rapid spread of Islam, and the unsealing of the hearts that were sealed to the truth for twenty years due to the resistance of the Qurayshi disbelievers following the conquests of Mecca and Taif.

---

[15] *Sahih al-Bukhari*, Tafsir as-Surah 110/3

[16] *Sahih al-Bukhari*, Tafsir as-Surah 110/3; Alusi, *Ruhu'l-Ma'ani*, 30/326

Bukhari reported that Amr ibn Salamah said: When Mecca was conquered, every tribe hastened to declare their acceptance of Islam the Messenger of Allah, all of the tribes were waiting for the conquest to accept Islam saying, if he prevails over them he will be a Prophet. The objective of the word "victory" in the surah is, as a majority agree, the conquest of Mecca, but also the victory of conquering the hearts, the hearts becoming unsealed to the religion of truth and the gates of Islam opening to the whole of humanity. The corporal and spiritual conquests of Islam that spread throughout Arabia and the universe initially began with the opening of the doors to the Ka'ba.

According to Mawdudi, "victory" here does not imply victory in any one particular campaign but the decisive victory after which there remained no power in the land to resist and oppose Islam, and it became evident that Islam alone would hold sway in Arabia. Some commentators have taken this to imply the Conquest of Mecca. But the conquest of Mecca took place in A.H. 8, and this surah was revealed towards the end of A.H.10. Besides, the statement of Abdullah ibn Abbas that this is the last surah of the Qur'an to be revealed, also goes against this commentary. For if the victory implied the conquest of Mecca, the whole of Surah at-Tawbah was revealed after it so this could not be the last surah. There is no doubt that the conquest of Mecca was decisive in that it broke the power of the Arabian pagans, yet even after this, they showed clear signs of resistance. The battles of Taif and Hunayn were fought after it, and it took Islam about two years to attain complete control over Arabia.

When the time for the people to enter Islam in one's and two's comes to an end, and when whole tribes and people belonging to large tracts start entering it in crowds, of their own free will, and without offering battle or resistance. This happened from the beginning of A.H. 9, and due to this that year has been described as "the year of deputations." Deputations from every part of Arabia started coming before the Holy Messenger, entering Islam and taking the oath of allegiance to him, until when he went for the Farewell Pilgrimage to Mecca, in A.H. 10, the whole of Arabia had become Muslim, and not a single polytheist remained anywhere in the country.

2. وَرَأَيْتَ النَّاسَ يَدْخُلُونَ فِي دِينِ اللهِ أَفْوَاجًا *"And you see people entering Allah's Religion in throngs."*

The word "entering" rather than "entered" in the declaration and you see people entering signifies that not all have entered, but that they have begun to enter, and will do so gradually. "Nas" (people) includes nations other than Arabs, and those who will enter in the future. In other words, they are entering, will continue to enter the Islamic faith, and in such numbers.

"Afwaj": in crowds, in groups. After the conquest of Mecca, in the two years following the Battle of Hunayn and the invasion of Taif until the death of the Prophet, groups from the entire Arabian Peninsula came and embraced Islam, and those who did not become Muslims accepted the Islamic Covenant and became nationals of the Islamic State. You see people entering Allah's religion in throngs,

3. فَسَبِّحْ بِحَمْدِ رَبِّكَ وَاسْتَغْفِرْهُ إِنَّهُ كَانَ تَوَّابًا *"Then glorify your Lord with His praise, and ask Him for forgiveness; for He surely is One Who returns repentance with liberal forgiveness and additional reward."*

In this surah, Allah informs His Prophet that when Islam has reached victory, and the people begin to embrace Islam in groups, his mission has come to an end. Then He commands the Prophet to glorify his Lord with praise and ask forgiveness, because by the favor of Allah, he had completed this great mission with huge success.

In this surah, it commands the Prophet to glorify his Lord with praise and ask forgiveness when Allah's help and victory comes, and he sees the people embracing Islam in groups. The addressee her is the Prophet, but his actions are an example for all believers, so in view of this, when a believer is granted the help and favor of Allah, it is his duty to glorify and praise Allah.

Another important point here is the difference between a Prophet and a temporal leader. If a temporal leader is successful in introducing reforms in this world, he will take pride and glory in his accomplishment by organizing ceremonies and celebrations. But here, although there is a Prophet who transformed the belief, perception, ethics, culture, civilization, social relations, concept of war and economy of a nation overwhelmed with ignorance, and exalted this nation to the position capable of ruling the entire world and worthy of leading all the nations of the world; rather than celebrating this great accomplishment, he was commanded to glorify and praise Allah, and ask His forgiveness.

Glorification is regarding Allah free from all deficiencies. As conveyed by interpreters of the Qur'an, when the Prophet was questioned regarding *tasbih* (glorification), he replied: "Allah the Almighty is free from all defects and deficiencies."[17] In which case, this defines the purity of Allah's Attributes, His actions and Names. According to Abussu'ud, it is "Praising the Lord by saying Glory be to Allah."

Here, the meaning of praise is: "It should not occur to you even for a moment that this major accomplishment is the result of your own capability. This success materialized by the favor of Allah alone. Therefore, praise Allah and acknowledge this in your speech and in your hearts, for the One who materialized such a great mission and created the foundation for this success is Allah alone, He is the only One worthy of praise."

Another meaning of the word "glorification" is: "Allah is not in need of your efforts for the exaltation of His words. So acknowledge this. You must certainly believe that you only attain success in your efforts by the confirmation and help of Allah. Allah can grant accomplishment to any servant He wishes. Granting a duty of this kind to His servant is a gift, a favor. His favor upon you means granting you the honor of serving your religion." In addition, there is the aspect of proclaiming "Glory be to Allah" at the time of surprise or astonishment. When an unimaginable event occurs, people

---

[17] *Sunan ibn Majah*, Iqama, 179; Ahmad ibn Hanbal, *Musnad*, 5/384; Alusi, *Ruhu'l-Ma'ani*, XV, 2/329

say "Glory be to Allah" (*Subhanallah*). The meaning of this is that only Al-lah beholds the power to create such an astonishing act, no other force has the power to accomplish this."

وَاسْتَغْفِرْهُ إِنَّهُ كَانَ تَوَّابًا " "...*ask Him for forgiveness; for He surely is One Who returns repentance with liberal forgiveness and additional reward*."

Tawbah; is the repentance of sin and determination not to repeat that sin. Whereas *istighfar*; is seeking forgiveness from Allah. Nobody can repent for others, however, an individual can ask forgiveness for others. In the Qur'an, there are many excellent examples of this such as *"Our Lord! For-give me, and my parents, and all the believers, on the Day on which the Reckoning will be established"* (Ibrahim 14:41). Therefore, the command here وَاسْتَغْفِرْهُ is not addressed at the Prophet alone, but also for his follow-ers, in fact more so for his followers because Allah protected His Messenger from sin. In which case, the Prophet seeking forgiveness; was to teach the people the importance of asking forgiveness; for his followers to seek the forgiveness of Allah, and in respect of continual spiritual progress, consider-ing the previous status that was insufficient in comparison with the present.

In a report by the Prophet's dear wife Aisha, during the final stage of his life, the Prophet repeated the words "Subhanallahi wa bihamdih; ast-aghfirullah wa atubu ilayh" (Glory be to Allah and praise Him; I ask for-giveness from Allah, and turn to Him in repentance) frequently, and when she inquired about this, he said: "My Lord has informed me of a sign that I will see in my followers, and commanded me to glorify Him with praise and ask His forgiveness when I see it."[18]

It was also prescribed to ask Allah's forgiveness three times after the obligatory Prayers, after the Tahajjud Prayer (in the last third of the night), and for the pilgrims on completion of the hajj. It was also reported that ask-ing forgiveness was prescribed after performing the ritual of purification and at the end of a gathering. Whenever the Prophet departed from any gath-

---

[18] *Sahih Muslim*, Salah, 221; *Sunan an-Nasa'i*, Sarik, 3; *Sunan ibn Majah*, Hudud, 29; D -rimi, Riqaq, 15; Ahmad ibn Hanbal, *Musnad*, 2/282, 341, 450; 6/35,77,184

ering he would say: "Subhanakallahumma wa bihamdik; astaghfiruka wa atubu ilayk."[19]

It was narrated that when this surah was revealed, the Prophet delivered a sermon and said: "Allah gave one of His servants the choice between this world, and what He has with Him, and the servant chose what He has with Him."[20] Abu Bakr realized the meaning of this, and said we sacrifice our lives, wealth, families and children for you. In another report: When the Prophet recited this surah, the Companions rejoiced, but Abbas, may Allah be pleased with him, wept. The Messenger of Allah asked him "Why are you weeping uncle?" he replied "This is giving the news of your death." The Prophet answered "Yes, it is."[21]

---

[19] *Sahih Muslim*, Salah, 218–220

[20] *Sahih al-Bukhari*, Manakibu'l-Ansar, 45

[21] *Sahih al-Bukhari*, Tafsir as-Surah 110/3

SURAH AL-MASAD

بِسْمِ اللهِ الرَّحْمٰنِ الرَّحِيمِ

تَبَّتْ يَدَا أَبِي لَهَبٍ وَتَبَّ ۞ مَا أَغْنَى عَنْهُ مَالُهُ وَمَا كَسَبَ ۞ سَيَصْلَى نَارًا

ذَاتَ لَهَبٍ ۞ وَامْرَأَتُهُ حَمَّالَةَ الْحَطَبِ ۞ فِي جِيدِهَا حَبْلٌ مِنْ مَسَدٍ ۞

Interpretation

In the Name of Allah, the All-Merciful, the All-Compassionate,

1. May both hands of Abu Lahab be ruined, and ruined are they!
2. His wealth has not availed him, nor his gains.
3. He will enter a flaming Fire to roast;
4-5. And his wife, carrier of firewood, Around her neck will be a halter of strongly twisted rope.

This surah is also called Surah "al-Masad" or "Lahab." It is one of the surahs revealed during the early days of the Meccan period. It relates the destruction due to enmity and hostility against religion, in particular Abu Lahab which means "flame" and his wife, the enemies of Islam who entered the flames of suffering in this world before entering Hell, the eternal abode of flames. Abu Lahab's fate, and the fact that he would die in the state of disbelief was declared many years before.

The reason for its revelation

Bukhari, Tirmidhi and many other sources of the Prophetic traditions report from a narration by Ibn Abbas that when the verse *"And warn your nearest kinsfolk*" (ash-Shuara 26:214) was revealed, the Prophet proclaimed "O people, awaken to the calamity of the morning!"

The people asked "Who is saying?" and began to gather around him.

The Prophet asked them: "If I were to tell you that the enemy on horseback was waiting to attack, would you believe me?"

They replied: "We have never heard anything from you but the truth."

The Prophet said: "Then I warn you that you are heading for a grave torment."

Whereupon Abu Lahab said: "May you perish! Did you gather us for this?" and then stood up. Following this, Surah al-Masad was revealed.[22]

According to some reports, after saying this, Abu Lahab picked up a stone with the intention of throwing it at the Prophet. In a narration by Ibn Abbas, it relates: "When Abu Lahab reached the gathering of the Quraysh he said 'Muhammad is promising certain things, he believes these will transpire after death, so what is my gain?' and blowing the dust from his hands said, "Tabban lakuma" (May you perish), I do not see you have anything Muhammad pledges. It was reported that after this event Surah al-Masad was revealed."[23]

After the revelation of this surah and the Prophet conveyed the curse against his uncle, everyone abandoned all hope of compromising with the Prophet regarding faith. Because after saying this to his own uncle, it appeared almost impossible that the Messenger of Allah could come to any kind of agreement with anyone else regarding the subject of faith. A stranger who accepted Islam was closer to the Prophet than his own family, and those who persisted in disbelief were strangers even if they were his blood relatives.

Commentary

1. تَبَّتْ يَدَا أَبِي لَهَبٍ وَتَبَّ *"May both hands of Abu Lahab be ruined, and ruined are they!"*

---

22 Suyuti, *Durru'l-Mansur*, 8/665
23 *Sahih al-Bukhari*, Janaiz, 98

When the past tense verb "tabbat," which derives from the word "taba'ab" is used as a supplication it means to be perished, to be subjected to destruction. As a supplication, to express that they deserve grief and destruction it means to consider shameful, to condemn. "Tabban laka" and similar terms are used to reproach, to condemn like "May you perish" This is why the interpretation "May your hands perish" is quite common.

Despite the fact that he was granted the honor of possessing such a superior lineage as the Prophet's, and privileged to be the Prophet's uncle; because Abu Lahab rejected faith and persisted in his disbelief and enmity towards the Prophet, he perished. If these family ties, this honor was insufficient in saving Abu Lahab from such a fate, then the suffering, the misery of the others who loathed and abused the Prophet, who never repented for their actions is a warning to all.

Although the real name of the Prophet's uncle was Abdul Uzzah, the reason why was he called Abu Lahab was because his face was a reddish color. "Lahab" means the flame of fire. "Abu Lahab" means a face as bright as a flame. There are several reasons why he was referred to by this nickname: The first is that he was recognized more by that nickname than he was his own name. Secondly, his name was Abdul Uzzah (the servant of Uzzah), the name of an idol, thus the Qur'an did not want to refer to him by the name of an idol. Thirdly, as his fate is revealed in this surah, it was more appropriate to mention him by this nickname, because Arabs referred to an evil person as "Abu Shar" and a righteous person as "Abu Khayr."

As we mentioned above, the first verb is a curse: may the hands of Abu Lahab perish, may he be destroyed. The second verb "wa tabb" is to notify of an event. It affirms that Abu Lahab was in fact ruined, that he was subjected to destruction and defeat. The meaning of "hand" here is actually the owner. This is an expression related according an Arab custom. By saying a certain part or fragment of something, they in fact mean the entirety of that object/subject. In other words, Abu Lahab himself was subjected to destruction. He perished before reaching his objective. Abu Lahab was inflicted by a fatal disease known as "adasa" which is similar to smallpox, and died seven days after hearing the news of the Quraysh' defeat in the Battle of Badr. According to reports by Alusi and other scholars, because the Quraysh avoided the "adasa" disease like it was the plague, even the members of his family would not go anywhere near him, thus his body was left to decompose for three days. Eventually, due to the fact that they felt ashamed of their actions, his family hired a few Abyssinian men to bury him. In another report, they dug a grave and pushed his body into it with long pieces of wood, and then threw stones onto his body until the grave was completely covered. According to another narration, they did not dig a hole, but placed him beneath a wall and casted stones at him until his body was totally covered.

2. مَا أَغْنَى عَنْهُ مَالُهُ وَمَا كَسَبَ *"His wealth has not availed him, nor his gains."*

According to some, the meaning of the word "gains" in this verse is Abu Lahab's children. In one of the traditions, it relates: "The purest thing comes from your own earnings, and your children are from your earnings."[24] While according to others, their reward is from the acts they perform on the presumption that they are fulfilling a favor. This is the meaning of the following verse: "*And We will turn to deal with all the deeds that they did, and will reduce them all to dust particles scattered about*" (al-Furqan 25:23). Abu Lahab was reported to have said "Even if what my nephew says is true, I will save myself from the painful torment on the Day of Judgment with my wealth and my children."

During Abu Lahab's illness, neither his wealth nor children were of avail to him, they abandoned him to death. Even his sons were not even granted the dignity of burying the body of their father in an honorable manner. Thus, within only a few years after the revelation of this surah, everyone witnessed how the fate of Abu Lahab materialized.

3. سَيَصْلَى نَارًا ذَاتَ لَهَبٍ *"He will enter a flaming Fire to roast."*

---

24 *Sunan Abu Dawud*, Buyu, 77

These are extremely fierce flames, like nothing that has ever been seen in this world. It is not only a fire which burns objects, but a fire of Hell which encompasses the souls and penetrates the hearts.

4. وَامْرَأَتُهُ حَمَّالَةَ الْحَطَبِ *"And his wife, carrier of firewood."*

In other words, Abu Lahab will not be cast into the fire alone, but together with his wife. His wife, Umm Jamil was the daughter of Harb and the sister of Abu Sufyan ibn Harb. She will also enter Hellfire as the carrier of firewood. As she assisted him in his disbelief and hostility in this world, she will assist to increase his torment and punishment by enhancing the flames in Hell, because this woman was as evil as her husband in her acts of hostility towards the Prophet.

The words "hammalat al-hatab" here literally means the "carrier of fire wood." According to reports, late at night, Abu Lahab's wife would scatter thorns on the ground in front of the Prophet's home and on the path he walked in order to cause him suffering, and this is why she was condemned in this manner.

According to some; his wife would carry tales to conspire against him. Thus, she was referred to in Arabic as the "woman who carried firewood," because the Arabs call those who kindle the flames of mischief "carriers of firewood."

5. فِي جِيدِهَا حَبْلٌ مِنْ مَسَدٍ *"Around her neck will be a halter of strongly twisted rope."*

In Arabic, the word "jid" means a neck decorated with an ornament, or a neck worthy of adornment. Umm Jamil wore a valuable necklace and said: "By Lat and Uzzah, I will sell this necklace and use the money to satisfy my hostility against Muhammad." Therefore, the word "jid" in this case, is used as a form of sarcasm. In other words, the neck on which you wore a necklace and boasted of will have a rope around it in Hell.

The word "masad" means fiber. In Arabic, everything twisted into rope form with fibers or date leaves is called *al-masad*. There will be a twisted and plated rope of strong fibers around her neck. As a result, *al-masad* means a strong rope of twisted date-palm fibers. Briefly, this verse means "there will be a strong rope of iron tied around her neck."

According to certain scholars; the words "carrier of firewood" was used as the means of defamation to signify her evil character. This evil woman who wore a necklace of twisted gold, will have a rope of flames tied around her neck in the Hereafter, thus, this will be an equal act of punishment.

The only people openly mentioned by name, condemned and considered worthy of eternal damnation in the Qur'an are Abu Lahab and his wife. This clearly indicates the extent of damage they caused to the Islamic mission, and how much grief they caused the Prophet.

Due to its relevance with the subject, I would like to add the answer to a question here:

Why does the Qur'an mention a person such as Abu Lahab, can you explain the wisdom this? How is this compliable with its eloquence?

Although he originated from the same linage Prophet Muhammad, peace and blessings be upon him, the source of light and guidance, Abu Lahab was one of the unfortunate, obstinate ones not granted the favor of benefitting from that guidance. His real name is Abdul Uzzah.

Briefly, the meaning of this surah is as follows: "May both hands of Abu Lahab be ruined, and ruined are they! His wealth has not availed him, nor his gains. He will enter a flaming Fire to roast; And his wife, carrier of firewood, Around her neck will be a halter of strongly twisted rope." He constantly used his will and determination to abuse, and to inflict evil. He scattered thorns on the Prophet's path and light fires on the roads leading to the Ka'ba. Naturally, his punishment will be equal to his evil actions, and he will go and enter the flames of Hell. Indeed, he was referred to as "Abu Lahab" which means the father of fire. This man who opposed the campaign for the exaltation, the spread of Islam, was to devise lies and schemes against the Prophet and Islam until the time of his death, and this is exactly what he did. But all of his plans and scheming failed. Despite the fact that the wealth of the Banu Umayya was passed onto Abu Lahab, and the fact that his wife Umm Jamil was a very wealthy woman, his wealth and possessions were of no avail. His sons were unable to save him, whereas these were the two things he boasted of the most.

Abu Lahab did not attend the Battle of Badr. When news of the Muslims victory at Badr reached Mecca, Abu Lahab became so angry. The one who brought news of the defeat related an unexpected occurrence, he said there were turbaned soldiers helping the Muslims. Abu Rafi, a man who concealed his faith, was among those listening to the news of the defeat. On hearing this, he was unable to contain his excitement any longer and exclaimed "By Allah, those were the angels." In a state of anger, Abu Lahab walked over to Abu Rafi and pushed him to the ground beating him continuously. Abu Rafi was Abbas's slave. Umm Fadl, Abbas's wife rushed over to Abu Lahab and struck him on the head with a wooden pole. She cried out "Why do you treat him like this, because his master is not here to protect him?" Abu Lahab ignored Umm Fadl, his brother's wife. He walked home with blood gushing from the wound on his head. He was infected with disease called "adasa" probably as a result of this wound which was considered to be more fatal than the plague at that time. Abu Lahab had children and wealth, but neither was of any avail to him. Alone he suffered great pain for seven days, and there was nobody with him when he died. His sons even refused to enter the house to remove the body. Eventually they felt ashamed of their actions, so they hired a few Bedouins from the desert to throw his decomposed body into a grave, and cast stones over the body.

Although he was such a close relative of the Prophet, not only had Abu Lahab refused to benefit from his guidance, but he became the Prophet's most brutal enemy. Thus, he was to suffer a horrific punishment both in this world and the Hereafter. He suffered his due punishment in this world, and he will certainly give account for his actions in the world beyond.

Abu Lahab's wife, Umm Jamil was a wealthy woman who came from the honorable family Banu Umayya. Her enmity towards the Messenger of Allah gave her great pleasure. She played a major role in many of the acts of persecution against the Prophet, and took immense pleasure in doing so. She collected thorns to scatter on the Prophet's path, carried wood to burn on the paths he walked, and enjoyed every minute of it. Although she was accustomed to a life of luxury and servants, her anger and hostility towards the Prophet provoked her to the extent that, she ignored her pride and position, and personally performed duties that were usually only done by slaves. While she would never lower herself in wearing anything but the best, most valuable jewelry, she now has a rope of twisted fibers around her neck and carries firewood on her back. In the Hereafter, she will suffer a punishment of the same kind she inflicted upon the Prophet in this world, as indeed, this is defined in the Qur'an.

Abu Lahab was an extremely stubborn man. Speaking of him, Abu Jahl said "Never anger him, if he joins the other side, nothing could make him return." And he was right. However, he consumed his stubbornness and determination in his enmity towards the Prophet. Abu Lahab and his wife worshipped the idols in the Ka'ba. They worshipped and named these idols, but not once did they display any effort in understanding the guidance of a man like the Prophet, who was brought up in their neighborhood and addressed the entire universe. Not once did they consider benefitting from this distinguished man, a mercy to the entire universe.

Rather than benefitting from his guidance, Abu Lahab displayed continuous cruelty and hostility towards the Prophet. Never did he abstain from these acts of wickedness, as his intention was constantly inflicting hardship. Abu Lahab joined Abu Jahl, the one who organized and lead the boycott against the Muslims that was to last for three years, and persecuted the Prophet and the Muslims. Throughout these three years the Muslims were on the verge of death. Many of the elderly and children died during this boycott. But their suffering never aroused the slightest emotion of compassion in the heart of Abu Lahab. He was a man who bore no conscience, no mercy. Unable to bear the cruelty any longer, the Prophet's dear wife Khadija, who was psychologically exhausted due to these hardships died in this year that was to be known as the "year of sorrow." Abu Talib, the Prophet's uncle also died in the same year. Unfortunately, he died before embracing Islam. However, due to his love for the Prophet, Abu Talib endured persecution and cruelty that only a believer could endure. When I hear the name Abu Talib, I experience a pain in the depth of my heart, my eyes fill with tears and I weep on many occasions. It is very sad that a man who helped and protected the Messenger of Allah to such an extent died in a state of disbelief. This is why Abu Bakr wept. One day, he brought his elderly father to the Prophet. His father, Abu Quhafah embraced Islam. In the meantime, Abu Bakr sat in a corner weeping. The Prophet asked: "O Abu Bakr! Why are you crying, you should rejoice for your father has embraced Islam?" He replied: "O Messenger of Allah! I would have been happier if Abu Talib accepted Islam as you loved Abu Talib more than Abu Quhafah." Indeed, we cannot show the impertinence of being more merciful than the Divine Compassion, however, I must say that find it difficult to control my heart. If only all of my rewards were given to Abu Talib and he was saved. Maybe it is wrong for me to speak in such a manner, but as I said previously, I cannot control my heart. Abu Talib protected the dear Prophet for many years, and endured great hardships for the sake of the Prophet. Neither I, nor anyone else has the right to say anything, because this is an obstacle that prevents the Prophet from helping him.

While Abu Talib protected and supported his nephew to such an extent, his brother Abu Lahab displayed acts of cruelty and persecution towards the Prophet. As the Prophet visited the Qurayshi tribes conveying Islam, the religion of truth and invited them to faith, a redheaded, red-bearded man followed him and constantly tried to contradict what the Prophet was saying, this redheaded man was Abu Lahab.

While members of tribes from afar came to establish a relationship and kinship with the Prophet, Abu Lahab considered it an incumbent duty to distance himself from his nephew. How could Abu Lahab not recognize the light of guidance, this ray of hope that was born and raised in his neighborhood?

Therefore, is this not a valid reason for the Qur'an declaring "May both hands of Abu Lahab be ruined." If he was not addressed in this manner, would the rights of millions of believers not have been lost? How else could a perception as such be conveyed in the language of the Qur'an which is full of wisdom and important topics?

Secondly: Both direct and indirect surahs were revealed regarding many who opposed and strived to damage Islam. Walid ibn Mughirah was one of those people. In the Qur'an, it says "Be away from Allah's mercy, how he calculated!" He was the father of Khalid ibn Walid. However, he was one of the most relentless enemies of the Prophet. He constantly schemed on how he could slander the Prophet: he hesitated on whether to call him a poet, a magician or a soothsayer. Eventually, he decided to call the Qur'an magic and the Prophet a sorcerer, and in the Qur'an, Allah responded to his decision by addressing Walid ibn Mughirah with the words: "Be away from Allah's mercy, how he calculated!"

Many other disbelievers were reproached and threatened in the Qur'an. In which case, if exceptions were made for Abu Lahab, could this have been in compliance with the fact that Qur'an is a universal Book? Of course not! If Walid ibn Mughirah had been reproached for his actions and Abu Lahab remained unpunished, then would this not have aroused the idea that, this man who had persecuted the Prophet to this extent, was only spared because of his family ties with the Messenger of Allah? But the Qur'an did not allow this to happen, and classified Abu Lahab as being in the same category as the other polytheists.

Thirdly: This surah was revealed in Mecca, and Abu Lahab died immediately after the Battle of Badr. In which case, this was a prediction from the world beyond. Abu Lahab and his wife were to die in the state of disbelief, and whatever the Qur'an stated became reality. In the same way that in Badr, the Prophet pointed to the particular places of where the leaders of the Quriash would die and each of them fell to their deaths on those predicted locations, an event which served to boost the spiritual morale of the believers. Similarly, the predicted death of Abu Lahab becoming a reality also gave the Muslims a spiritual boost, but in addition was virtually a warning, a caution to all believers. Indeed, everything the Qur'an pledged became a reality. There was a pledge of victory, so this would also come true. Support of this kind, and in a period in which everyone behave like an enemy of this small group of believers was certainly something that should not be underestimated. On the contrary, when we consider the outcome, in a sense this was undoubtedly a necessary part of the process.

Sometimes, the caution of warning that emerges from a small misfortune or calamity can add such dimension and attainment to spiritual life that, if the veil is removed, and these attainments are witnessed, everyone would want those misfortunes and calamities to reoccur, as these misfortunes are relatively small in comparison with the gains. Indeed, in the name of humanity, even if everything necessary was said regarding those who are doomed to loose, this would not change the outcome in the least. The damage was done and their terrible fate was inevitable. Although the miserable fate of a couple of individuals is mentioned in this surah, and may appear to some to be somewhat degrading to the honor of mankind, considering that as a result this lead to millions of people perceiving their own depths, or at least to reflect and avoid a terrible fate like those mentioned, the wisdom in this is sure to replace the initial impressions that came to mind. Undoubtedly, they will perceive the wisdom in the psychological and pedagogical terms of mentioning Abu Lahab and his wife in the Qur'an, and how necessary and beneficial this was for the believers.

Fourthly: Finally, we must add this point, just as the psychological effects of this surah was the means of awakening for those who believed, a sense of doubt began to generate among the disbelievers. By transforming their disbelief into doubt, accepting the path of light became easier, and due to these doubts the acknowledgment of faith that was previously confined in their conscious alone, began to penetrate their minds and hearts, and a short while after the fruits of this began to emerge. Then forsaking their disbelief, many were adorned in the gown of faith and began to guide others. In the name of faith and mankind, this was not something to be underestimated. Certainly, generating such tremendous results by relating the fates of certain individuals is a miraculous style consistent with the Qur'an, and evidence of its statements full of wisdom never accomplished by any other scripts. In a sense, this is like thousands of waves emerging from a tiny stone cast into the vast ocean with all its color and depth. Indeed, since that period, those waves had a continuous impact on the hearts of thousands, hundreds of thousands and even millions of individuals until today. The Qur'an, both with the appealing and unappealing aspects of advice and warning, was revealed in such a superior, sublime manner that from the time it stated that an individual would die in the state of disbelief, it was the means of millions of people embracing Islam. This conforms to the declarations of eloquence and clarity of the Qur'an, the epitome of guidance and wisdom.[25]

---

[25] Gülen, M. Fethullah, *Asrın Getirdiği Tereddütler*, Vol.3, pp.134–141

SURAH AL-IKHLAS

بِسْمِ اللهِ الرَّحْمٰنِ الرَّحِيمِ

قُلْ هُوَ اللهُ أَحَدٌ ۞ اَللهُ الصَّمَدُ ۞ لَمْ يَلِدْ وَلَمْ يُولَد ۞ وَلَمْ يَكُنْ لَهُ كُفُوًا أَحَدٌ ۞

Interpretation

In the Name of Allah, the All-Merciful, the All-Compassionate,

1. Say: "He (He is) Allah, the Unique One of Absolute Oneness.
2. Allah is the Eternally-Besought-of-All,
3. He begets not, nor is He begotten.
4. And comparable to Him there is none."

Al-Ikhlas, which was one of the first surahs to be revealed consists of four verses, and takes its name from the subject theme. Like al-Fatiha, this sublime surah also has many other names, the most common being "Ikhlas" and "Qul huwallahu." This surah was called "Al-Ikhlas" (The Purity) because it conveys the unification of Allah, the basis of the Islamic faith in the purest, most excellent manner. Allah the Almighty was never described so beautifully in any other scripts as He was in the Qur'anic scripts Ayat al-Kursi and Surah al-Ikhlas, or in any religion other than Islam. This surah rejects all kinds of polytheism in an extremely concise manner.

In addition, this surah was also referred to as "Surah at-Tawhid" (the Surah of Unification), "Surah at-Tafrid" (the Surah of Uniqueness), "Surah al-Najat" (the Surah of Salvation), "Surah al-Walayat" (the Surah of Guardianship) and "Surah al-Marifah" (the Surah of Gnosis), because those who fully understand this surah recognize Allah.

This surah was also called "Surah al-Nisbah" (the Surah of Linage), because according to a report by Tirmidhi, this surah was revealed after the polytheists told the Prophet "O Muhammad! Tell us the linage of your Lord." Thus, it was revealed that Allah is free from linage.[26]

It was also called "Surah as-Samad" and "Surah al-Muawwidah."

Abdullah ibn Unays said: "The Messenger of Allah placed his hand on my chest and said 'recite' but I did not know what to recite. Then he said 'Say: 'He is Allah, the Unique One of Absolute Oneness." So I recited the whole surah, then he said 'Say 'I seek refuge in the Lord of the daybreak." So I recited the surah until the end. Then he said 'Say 'I seek refuge in the Lord of humankind." So I completed this surah, then the Prophet said 'Seek refuge in Allah like this. None who seeks the refuge of Allah has ever sought His refuge like those who recite these three surahs.'"[27]

In a narration by Ibn Abbas, it was called "Surah al-Man'ia" (the Surah of Protection) because it protects against the torture of the grave. In one of the traditions, the Prophet said: "Everything has a light, and the light of the Qur'an is قُلْ هُوَ اللهُ أَحَدٌ. This was the reason why this surah was called "Surah an-Nur" (the Surah of Light).[28]

This surah was also called "Surah al-Aman" (the Surah of Safety) because when unification is non-existent, faith is not complete. As Surah al-Kafirun and this surah relate to one another in terms of the significance of the banishment and attestation of the word of unification, these two surahs together were referred to as the "Ikhlasayn surahs."

As for its revelation, there are two different opinions as to whether it was a Meccan or Medinan surah. Regarding the reason for its revelation, again there are two varying views due to two differing traditions; some settled the differing opinion of the two traditions by saying there was a repetition of the revelation. These two traditions relate two differing reports as to

---

[26] *Sunan at-Tirmidhi*, Tafsir as-Surah, 112/1, 2
[27] *Sunan an-Nasai*, Istiaza, 1
[28] Alusi, *Ruhu'l-Ma'ani*, XV, 2/341

whether the Jews or the polytheists were the reason for the revelation of this surah.

The reason for its revelation

Those who claim it was revealed in response to the polytheists narrate from Abu al-Aliyah on the authority of Ubay ibn Ka'b, and Sha'bi on the authority of Jabir. The polytheists asked the Prophet "Tell us the linage of your Lord." After which Allah revealed Surah al-Ikhlas. According to Ikrima, the polytheists said to the Prophet "Tell us about the attributes of your Lord, He who sent you as a Prophet" And as a result, Allah revealed the surah *"Say: 'He is Allah, the Unique One of Absolute Oneness.'"*

Those who say it was in response to a question from the Jews narrated this report: A group of Jews came to the Prophet and said, "O Muhammad! Allah created mankind, but who created Allah?" Upon hearing this, the Prophet became extremely angry, and rebuked them for asking such a question. Then Jibril came and said: "O Muhammad! Your Lord has sent an answer to their question. Convey to them *"Say: 'He is Allah, the Unique One of Absolute Oneness.'"*

In a report by Qatadah, a group of Jews came to the Prophet and said "Inform us of the ancestry of your Lord." Upon which the surah *"Say: 'He is Allah, the Unique One of Absolute Oneness'"* was revealed.[29]

According to a narration by Imam ar-Razi, this surah was revealed following the questions put forth by the Christians.[30] Ata narrated from Ibn Abbas: A Christian delegation that came from Najran asked us to describe our Lord "What is He made from, what substance is He made from?" The Messenger of Allah replied "My Lord is not created from anything, He is the Creator of all things." Then the surah *"Say: 'He is Allah, the Unique One of Absolute Oneness'"* was revealed.

The time or period of the surahs regarding which there is no question of abrogation, bears no great significance. Knowledge of whether a surah is

---

[29]   Suyuti, *Durru'l-Mansur*, 8/670
[30]   Ar-Razi, Fakhr ad-Din, *Tafsir al-Kabir*, 32/175

Meccan or Medinan in terms of the reason for its revelation does not
change the result or the judgment of the surah. Learning the reason for the
revelation of such surahs is simply to clarify the place of its revelation and
identify the situation in which it was revealed. As a result, there is no doubt
that in addition to all forms of polytheism, this surah also rejects the Christian belief of the trinity.

Commentary

1. قُلْ هُوَ اللهُ أَحَدٌ **"Say: 'He is Allah, the Unique One of Absolute**
   Oneness.'"

The initial addressee of this surah is the Prophet, then every believer is
its addressee. As the command is expressed so clearly, it emphasizes that
this is a Divine statement and there is warning that this must be recited and
conveyed word for word. In other words, by accepting that what Allah reveals as the word of truth without any doubt in the heart and confessing
this with the tongue, convey this to others how you affirmed it yourself.
This is a duty of all believers.

Allah is One, He is unique.

Although the word "Ahad" is also used for "Wahid" meaning one,
there is a significant difference between the two. Oneness is the most elo-
quent definition meaning of He is the One and only. The word "Wahid" or
one can be used in the relative and nominal sense, and expresses a numeral significance. "Ahad" means absolute oneness, unique, and is used about
something uncountable, that which does not accept numerousness, the true
One of which there is no other, which is and will always be One. Therefore, the words "Wahid" and "Ahad" do not bear the same meaning.

"Ahad" means unique, the one and only; Ahad is one of the Names of
Allah that belongs to Him alone. Nothing can be associated with Him.

In brief, it means "Allah is One," in whatever way we approach this, in
His Holy Essence, His Attributes or His Names, He is Unique, the One who
has no partners. Divineness is His alone. The Oneness of Allah is not referring to one in the numeric terms as in two divided by two. The Oneness of

Allah is oneness that is unique in every sense, a oneness that rejects partnership or duality in every aspect.

Allah is One, is Unique in every respect. "Allah existed and nothing else existed with Him, and now Allah exists and nothing else exists with Him." Imam al-Azam Abu Hanifa mentioned this in his work *Al-Fiqh al-Akbar* with the words "Allah is One not in numeral sense, but in the sense that He has no partners."

2. الله الصَّمَدُ "*Allah is the Eternally-Besought-of-All.*"

In other words, "Allah is independent of everything, and everything is dependent upon Him." He is One, the Sustainer, the Almighty Lord who is the absolute essence of everything, the One upon who everyone is dependent for their needs and requests. Indeed, He is the most perfect, the only One who is Eternal (As-Samad).

It was reported that Abu Hurayra said: "Allah is independent of all, but all are dependent on Him."[31]

As-Samad also has other meanings:

1. The One who is appealed to in every matter, is sought refuge in; without whose command nothing can happen, the One who is obeyed.
2. The One who is independent, who does not eat or drink.
3. Something which is solid, with no holes or emptiness.
4. The Lord whose lordship has reached its peak.

There is vast meaning in this sentence. Indeed, the word "As-Samad" is recognition of Allah. Therefore, when you say "As-Samad," the truth that you perceive, acknowledge and imply is unique to Allah in every aspect. In which case, no one but Allah can be called As-Samad.

The word "samad" may be used as a common noun regarding humans. Therefore, those other than Allah may be referred to as "samad" in any aspect. This is why the leader of a tribe is called "samad al-kawm."

3. لَمْ يَلِدْ وَلَمْ يُولَد "*He begets not, nor is He begotten.*"

---

[31] Alusi, *Ruhu'l-Ma'ani*, XV,2/351

He begets not, meaning He did not father another. Nor is He begotten, in other words, He was not born, given birth to. He is eternal and did not come into existence after, but existed since past eternity. In the same way that Allah is not the father of children, He is not the son of another. Just as Allah is not a father or begetter, nor is He a son or begotten; this is neither probable nor feasible, but is totally impossible. Indeed, as the one who begets is mortal and dependent, the begotten is by no means independent and is not eternally existent.

The word "lam yalid" refutes the act of begetting, and "wa lam yulad" eliminates being a son or fathered. Because the Christian doctrine of the trinity claims that the father is Allah, then the son is Allah, and that the father obviously comes before the son, whereas "He begets not" was revealed first in this surah and then "Nor is He begotten" particularly to refute this claim.

This surah rejects all those who attribute offspring to Allah. For example the Jews who said "*Ezra (Uzayr) is Allah's son*" (at-Tawbah 9:30) and the Christians who say "*The Messiah is Allah's son*" (at-Tawbah 9:30) and the Arab polytheists who "*...assign daughters to Allah*" (an-Nahl 16:57). By revealing that He begets not, Allah the Almighty denied all of these. As a child has to be the same species as his father, whereas Allah is unique Allah is eternal, He has no beginning or end. Therefore, it is impossible for Him to have children. In addition to this, only those who have a spouse can have children, and Allah has no spouse because He is One, He is unique in every sense, there is none of His kind, no equal that He may have offspring. Thus, this is emphasized in the following verse of the Qur'an "*The Originator of the heavens and the earth with nothing before Him to imitate. How can He have a child, when there is for Him no consort...*" (al-An'am 6:101).

He is neither the son of a father or mother, as everything that is born comes into existence later, whereas Allah is eternal, He existed in pre-eternity, He existed when nothing else existed. In which case it is impossible that Allah was begotten.

4. وَلَمْ يَكُنْ لَهُ كُفُوًا أَحَدٌ *"And comparable to Him there is none."*

"Kufuw" means being the same in level and value, in other words, it means the same or equal, which can also mean the equivalent or similar. In terms of glory and worthiness, there is no existence that is equal to Allah in any way. There has never been any equivalent to Allah in His essence, in His attributes or His acts; no equal, partner or competitor to oppose or contradict His Uniqueness, and there never will be. In the same way that there was never any equal to Him in the past, there never will be in the future. There is no "Wajib al-Wujud" or "Necessary Existence" other than Allah. Because there never has been in the past, it is impossible for there to be in the future, and because those who come into existence later are descendants or creatures, it is impossible for them to be of His equal in any sense. Therefore, the entire universe and its content, the skies and earth, the objective and subjective worlds, the spirit and body, the material and physical, space and time, the Divine Throne and the heavens, the universe and the Hereafter together are not equal to Allah. Indeed, Allah was existent when none of these existed, He was the One who created all of these.

Everything may have an equal, an equivalent, a partner or an opponent, as it was revealed in the Qur'an *"And all things We have created in pairs..."* (adh-Dhariyat 51:49). Only Allah has no partner or equal, and never will.

In one of the Sacred Traditions (Hadith Qudsi) it relates: "The son of Adam disbelieves in Me though he ought not and he abuses Me though he has no right. As for his disbelieving in Me, it is his statement that He will not be resurrected as was created, though his recreation is easier for Me than the first creation. As for his abusing Me, it is him saying that Allah has a son, but I am the One, the Eternal. I have neither begotten nor have been begotten nor do I have any match."[32]

Traditions conveying the virtues of Surah al-Ikhlas:

In many traditions narrated from the Prophet and the Companions, the Surah al-Ikhlas is reported to be equal to a third of the Qur'an. The noble Prophet said: "Is it difficult for any of you to recite one third of the Qur'an

---

[32] *Sahih al-Bukhari*, Tafsir as-Surah, 112

in one night?" One of the Companions said it would be difficult, upon which the Prophet said, "Reciting Surah al-Ikhlas is equal to reciting one third of the Qur'an."[33]

In another report the Prophet said: "Whoever recites Surah al-Ikhlas once, it is like he recited a third of the Qur'an, if he reads it twice it is as if he has recited two thirds of the Qur'an, and if he recited it three times, it is as if he has recited the whole of the Qur'an."[34] There are many similar reports.

So what does this mean? There are two different views of interpreters and Islamic scholars:

1. Some scholars claim that this is not in terms of reward, but in terms of meaning. Because the Qur'an is based upon three sciences: The science of "tawhid" (unification), the science of Sharia (Islamic law) and the science of "akhlaq" (Islamic ethics). This surah expresses both the sciences of Islamic law and ethics which is the foundation of the science of unification in the clearest, most excellent manner.

In addition, it was also said that knowledge in the Qur'an is divided into three: The verses that testify to the unity of Allah, the verses of Islamic commands and verses conveying examples of advice and warning. This chapter is classified as a third of the Qur'an because it contains verses testifying to the unity of Allah.

2. Some scholars said this surah is equal to a third of the Qur'an in terms of reward, and claimed that this was the meaning apparent in the traditions.

Although there were some who did not regard one surah being classified as superior to another acceptable and those who contest the difference in virtue of certain surahs, in view of the many traditions regarding this subject, it is surprising that they contest the superiority of this surah. Because the meaning of guidance such as the unity of Allah and the Divine Attributes Surah al-Ikhlas contains is not found in Surah al-Masad. So conse-

---

[33] *Sahih al-Bukhari*, Ayman, 3
[34] *Sahih Muslim*, Musafirin, 259

quently, superiority is only associated with the sublimity and vastness of meaning.

Surahs which affirm the sublime names and attributes of Allah; that signify His magnificence and glory in comparison with the other surahs are classified as superior in terms of being greater in value and glory.

Additionally, a surah may be called superior in these terms; if Allah rendered the recitation of a surah many times greater than other surahs, and granted reward for its recital He never granted for others. However, we do not know the true explanation or the reason for this degree of value or reward. As the like was said in terms of the superiority of time and space, true worship is that performed for the pleasure of Allah. In brief, any of these aspects regarding superiority is not inconsistent with the equality the Divine Scripts bear in terms of being the Word of Allah and bearing the same characteristics.

The Prophet told one of his Companions who recited this surah in every Prayer: "Your Love of this surah will lead you to Paradise."[35]

---

[35] *Sunan at-Tirmidhi*, Fadalilu'l-Qur'an, 11

SURAH AL-FALAQ

بِسْمِ اللهِ الرَّحْمٰنِ الرَّحِيمِ

قُلْ أَعُوذُ بِرَبِّ الْفَلَقِ ۞ مِنْ شَرِّ مَا خَلَقَ ۞ وَمِنْ شَرِّ غَاسِقٍ إِذَا وَقَبَ ۞

وَمِنْ شَرِّ النَّفَّاثَاتِ فِي الْعُقَدِ ۞ وَمِنْ شَرِّ حَاسِدٍ إِذَا حَسَدَ ۞

Interpretation

In the Name of Allah, the All-Merciful, the All-Compassionate,

1. Say: "I seek refuge in the Lord of the daybreak
2. From the evil of what He has created;
3. And from the evil of the darkness (of night) when it overspreads
4. And from the evil of the witches who blow on knots;
5. And from the evil of the envious one when he envies."

This surah was given its title from the word "falaq" found in the first verse meaning daybreak, and comprises of five verses. It teaches the people how to seek the refuge of Allah, and the means of attaining His protection.

Commentary

1. قُلْ أَعُوذُ بِرَبِّ الْفَلَقِ **"Say: 'I seek refuge in the Lord of the daybreak.'"**

The words *a'udh*, *ma'adh*, *iyadh* and *isti'adh* mean to seek refuge in another to protect oneself from evil, to ask protection. The act of seeing refuge consists of three factors: The first, the act of seeking refuge, the one who seeks refuge, and the One whose refuge is being sought. "Seeking refuge" means to rely on another for protection due to fear, to seek protection. The one who "seeks refuge" feels the necessity of seeking the protection of another because he is afraid of something and is not strong enough to fight it. The seeker of refuge believes that the one in whom he seeks refuge has the power to fight against and protect him from whatever he is afraid of.

The word *qul* "say" at the beginning of the surah is a part of the revelation. It is a part of the message of the Messenger of Allah's Prophethood. Although the Prophet is the initial addressee, this word is addressing every believer.

The reason for the word Rabb (Lord) being used in the verse and not Allah; is because seeking refuge in the Lord, the "One who disciplines," who "teaches" is more appropriate for seeking His protection.

بِرَبِّ الْفَلَقِ "In the Lord of the daybreak." The Creator of that daybreak; the One who gives life to the dead and gives death to the living, the One who splits the darkness and causes the daybreak to appear.

"Falaq" means to split and bring into existence. Here, very likely the word *falaq* means the daybreak which emerges with the split in the darkness of the night; in other words the rays of light which extend like a pillar into the skies, or the dawn appearing on the horizon. This is also called twilight. A majority of the interpreters of the Qur'an considered the interpretation to be the commonly used daybreak. According to this, "Rabbi'l-falaq" is the Lord of the morning, or in other words the Lord of the daybreak. *Rabbi'l-falaq* means *Faliqu'l-isbah* or He who causes the dawn to appear. In the same way that one who is in darkness awaits the light of dawn, he who is subjected to fear awaits salvation and the dawning of the light of achievement. The light of daybreak follows the darkness of night, and this signifies that after force there is an opening. However, this can mean everything that Allah created by splitting: The plantation that emerges with the splitting of the earth, the springs which flow from between the mountains, the rain that pours from amidst the clouds, the offspring born from the mother's womb, the buds that emerge from seeds, in brief, the word *falaq* includes the entire creation.

The reason for the using Rabb (Lord) rather than His proper Name Allah here is because Rabb, the "One who disciplines," who "teaches" is more appropriate for seeking His protection. If we consider the meaning of "Rabbi'l-falaq" to be "The Lord who causes the dawn to appear," then the meaning of this surah would be "I seek refuge in the Lord who causes the daybreak to emerge from darkness, the Lord who causes the prosperity of day to emerge from the calamity of the darkness." Another meaning is; the discipline that relieves of dangers. The Lord embraces those who seek refuge with Him and those who fear Him. In brief, He is the Lord of the people, and creation seek refuge in Him and fear Him because He is the Lord of the universe.

2. مِنْ شَرِّ مَا خَلَقَ *"From the evil of what He has created"*

In other words, from everything created by Allah; from the evil of any creation that may cause harm, and this includes all kinds of evil, material physical, pertaining to this world and the Hereafter, the objecting and subjective, the voluntary and involuntary. In which case, this includes the evil of everything that may be harmful from the evil of humans, jinn and the devil, from the evil of beasts of prey, insects, vermin and disease, from the evil of venom and fire, the evil of sin and desires, to the evil of the ego and of actions.

3. وَمِنْ شَرِّ غَاسِقٍ إِذَا وَقَبَ *"And from the evil of the darkness when it overspreads"*

"Ghasiq" is a word that has been interpreted in many different ways and has vast meaning. Many of the scholars, who interpreted "falaq" as meaning daybreak or morning, interpreted this as night or darkness, and "waqab" (wuqub) as the intense darkness to overspread completely. Darkness is specifically mentioned because this is the time when that evil begins to spread. Indeed, a majority of sins and crimes are committed in the darkness of night. The harmful and poisonous animals and insects emerge in the darkness of night. Therefore, seeking protection in the refuge of Allah before evil begins to spread bears great significance. In this surah, it prescribes seeking refuge in Allah particularly from the evil and calamities that appears in the darkness of the night. Here, the subtlety of seeking refuge in Allah, the One who causes the light of daybreak to emerge from the evil of the darkness of night is extremely important.

Some scholars define "ghasiq" as the moon and "wuqub" as the eclipse of the moon or the last three days of the month, and indeed there is report in one of the traditions supporting this. It was reported from Aisha, the Prophet's dear wife: "One day the Prophet looked up at the moon and said "O Aisha! Seek refuge in Allah from its evil as it is the evil of the night that comes with the darkness."[36]

According to Mawdudi, the correct explanation of this tradition is as follows: As the moon rises at night, the meaning of the Prophet's words was "Seek Allah's refuge from the night, the time when the moon appears." Because the light of the moon would not be of much benefit for those who resist attackers, it would be more helpful to the criminals than it is to the victims.

The night is *ghasiq*, when the darkness embarks. The moon is *ghasiq* in the darkness. Allah has not specified which of these was meant, but generalized. Therefore, it was commanded to seek refuge from both of these which may be classified as *ghasiq* at the time of darkness.

4. وَمِنْ شَرِّ النَّفَّاثَاتِ فِي الْعُقَدِ *"And from the evil of the witches who blow on knots"*

In other words, from the evil of the women or societies who blow on the knots they make in rope or thread, or who attempt to place "knots" in the hearts of their victims by tying knots in a thread or rope and blowing on them.

"Naffathat" is what we refer to as "to blow," or to blow ones breaths upon something or someone.

"Uqad" is the plural of "uqdah." *Uqdah*, which means gathering something by tying its two ends, is a knot.

---

[36]   *Sunan at-Tirmidhi*, Tafsir as-Surah 113, 114-1; Ahmad ibn Hanbal, *Musnad*, 6/60

One of the interesting points here is that the word "naffathat" was used in the feminine plural form. So in terms of its conveyance in feminine form, there are three explanations regarding who this was referring to:

1. Evidently, by referring to women, this means "women who blow" (female sorcerers). There are two aspects of this: The first is that a majority of those who practiced sorcery were women. The other is that the influence of a woman's deceit on the determination and power of men, the effect a woman's luring speech and appeal has on the hearts can be so great that, even those who do not believe in sorcery and the like acknowledge the females influence on males. In which case, we can say these two opinions are intended at the same meaning.

2. If this is relating to "nufus" meaning human beings, which includes both male and female, then is means "those who blow" (sorcerers).

3. According to another opinion, this refers to groups or societies therefore meaning "societies who blow" or societies of sorcerers.

Is reciting prayers or surahs and blowing on a person permissible?

If there is no sorcery involved, in other words, if it is not intended for evil but is to protect from evil, to seek a cure from Allah for an illness or to seek Allah's protection from some kind of calamity, then reciting a prayer or verse of the Qur'an and blowing with a pure and sincere intention of seeking cure or protection is permissible as this is not intended to harm anyone or seek refuge in anyone else other than Allah. Above all, the commands: *"Say! 'I seek refuge'"* in these verses emphasizes the necessity of seeking refuge in Allah from everything. It is known that the Prophet performed *ruqyah* (supplications for protection and healing) on himself and on others, and that he also gave permission for others to practice this for these means. There are many examples of individuals who regained health, both spiritual and physical, by virtue of these supplications.

Undoubtedly, as instructed in these and in other surahs, supplicating for himself and for others by seeking refuge in Allah was not only permitted, but was commanded in the Islamic faith.

Awf ibn Malik Ashjai said: "We used to practice *ruqyah* prior to Islam, and we asked the Messenger of Allah: 'What is your opinion regarding this?' He replied: 'Present your *ruqyah* to me, there is no harm in this as long as it does not contain *shirk* (associating partners to Allah).'"[37]

The types of *ruqyah* that were prohibited are that of which the truth is unknown, and that which contains sorcery and acts of polytheism.

As it is understood from both the Qur'an and traditions of the Prophet, in the Islamic faith it is commanded to abstain from evil acts of sorcery such as blowing on knots, and delusions that can be damaging to belief and to the body both mentally and physically. This is why a majority of the scholars elaborated on sorcery, agreed that believers should abstain from *ruqyah* that involves any kind of sorcery, and classified reciting on knots tied on thread or rope as a form of magic.

In accordance with the tradition "For every disease there is a cure"[38] just as treatment is permissible by spiritual means for psychological illnesses and material means for physical diseases, quite naturally a complex remedy for a more complicated illness is also permissible, on the condition that the effects are recognized not from the means, but from Allah and while performing these individuals must abstain from all kinds of scheming, sorcery, falsehoods, deceit and causing harm.

Seeking refuge in Allah, pleading for a cure from Allah with a sincere intention and pure breaths by supplicating and breathing on the sufferer cannot be classified as a kind of sorcery. Thus, those who considered *ruqyah* to be permissible presented many traditions conveyed in books of authentic traditions as evidence.

1. It was reported that once, when the Prophet became ill, Jibril came; he recited and blew on him and said "I blow on you in the Name of Allah from everything that troubles you. May Allah restore you to health."[39]

---

[37] *Sahih Muslim*, Salam, 64; *Sunan Abu Dawud*, Tibb, 18
[38] *Sahih Muslim*, Salam, 59
[39] *Sahih al-Bukhari*, Tibb, 38

2. Aisha, the Prophet's dear wife reported: When one of us became ill, or the Prophet visited the sick he would touch them with his right hand and supplicate: "O Allah! Lord of mankind. Remove this disease and cure this person. You are the Curer. There is no cure but through You, Your cure leaves no disease or affliction."[40]

3. The Prophet would pray for his grandsons Hasan and Husayn with the words: "I seek refuge for you both in the perfect words of Allah from every evil, every devil and every creature," and he added: "Ibrahim used to supplicate to Allah for his sons Ismail and Ishaq in this way."[41]

4. It was reported by Uthman ibn Abu al-As al-Thaqafi: I was in pain, so I went to the Prophet and he told me: "Place your hand where you feel the pain in your body and say:

"In the Name of Allah three times, and say I seek refuge with Allah and with His Power from the evil that I find and that I fear." I did this and Allah restored my health."[42]

5. The Prophet would recite the last three surahs of the Qur'an (Surahs al-Ikhlas, al-Falaq and an-Nas) every night, blow on his hands and rub his hands over his face and body.[43] It was reported by the Prophet's dear wife Aisha in authentic books of Hadith: "When a member of the Prophet's family became ill, he would recite the last three surahs of the Qur'an and blow over them.[44] When he became seriously ill, I used to recite these surahs and rub his hands over his body hoping for its blessings."

Indeed, from these reports the conclusion is that: Although practicing *ruqyah* to gain spiritual and physical health on the condition that it does not contain acts of sorcery, requesting that others recite these surahs over us, seek refuge in Allah and supplicate on our behalf is not approved of.

According to Hanafi scholars: As long as a person believes that a cure is simply the means of gaining health, and that Allah is the only One who

---

[40] *Sahih al-Bukhari*, Marda, 20; Tibb 38, 40
[41] *Sahih al-Bukhari*, Anbiya, 10
[42] *Sunan Abu Dawud*, Tibb, 19
[43] *Sahih al-Bukhari*, Tibb, 39
[44] *Sahih al-Bukhari*, Maghazi, 83

can grant a cure, then there is no objection to seeking treatment. But it is wrong to believe that the cure or treatment is the provider of health.

In this case, it is apparent from this explanation that cure by reciting supplications and blowing over the body is neither a necessity of piety or a practice commanded in the Islamic faith as many believe it to be, but is rather an act that was permitted. The true act of devoutness is seeking refuge in Allah alone, supplicating directly to Allah and not requesting the mediation of anyone for supplications. It is permissible or even approvable for a believer to supplicate for another believer either in his presence or his absence, in fact because this is a religious duty, and in view of the hadith, "Supplication is the essence of worship."[45] Although there is no doubt whatsoever that supplication is the basis of worship, of religious duty; supplication is one thing, while reciting, blowing and anticipating a cure or relief from anyone but Allah is something totally different. Allah the Almighty commanded supplication *"Pray to Me, I will answer you"* (al-Mumin 40:60); *"And when (O Messenger) My servants ask you about Me, then surely I am near: I answer the prayer of the suppliant when he prays to Me..."* (al-Baraqah 2:186) and *"Say: 'My Lord would not care for you were it not for your prayer...'"* (al-Furqan 25:77). But forbade polytheism and praying to any other than Himself *"Say: 'I worship only my Lord and I do not associate anyone as partner with Him'"* (al-Jinn 72:20). In the same way, He taught the most beautiful prayers in the Qur'an and through His Messenger, and in these surahs (al-Falaq and an-Nas) commanded that the believers seek refuge in Him directly from all evil. As conveyed by the Prophet, this can be practiced every night and when required, a person should recite for himself with a pure intention and heart, should bot supplicate for his fellow believers and also encourage them to do so, and not deny the blessing of those who supplicate with a pure intention. However, despite the fact that Allah opens the gates of such supplication and acceptance to everyone, calls everyone to supplication, commands that everyone seeks refuge in Him directly, and rejects the reprehensible act of polytheism; those who

---

[45]   *Sunan at-Tirmidhi*, Dua, 1

abstain from directly supplicating, praying and seeking refuge by worshipping to Allah, and seek a mediator on the presumption "I cannot supplicate to Allah directly, I do not know what to say." appealing to someone else for help is certainly not a requirement of the Islamic faith, this is an act of ignorance. Such an expansive explanation on this subject is necessary because people are not aware of certain aspects, and consider the practice of *ruqyah* as being a necessity of faith. Every believer must be aware that the sole granter of success is Allah.

In which case, briefly: Although "uqad" (knots) can possibly have many probable meanings sensually, spiritually and metaphorically, because its true meaning is knot this is evidently the knots in a rope or thread. However, it is clear that this is not referring to blowing to tie or untie a knot in a thread, as it is obvious that all knots made in thread cannot be classified as an act of sorcery. So the objective here is not actually blowing on the knot, but is intended at sorcery. So, because we understand the verse النَّفَّاثَاتِ فِي الْعُقَد to be those who practice sorcery, in general this means seek refuge from the evil or male and female sorcerers. But the act of sorcery is not restricted to knots alone. Therefore, this can mean anything to do with sorcery which entails attempting to change or reverse the course of something, and this includes all of the meanings mentioned.

5. وَمِنْ شَرِّ حَاسِدٍ إِذَا حَسَدَ **"And from the evil of the envious one when he envies."**

"Hasad," or envy is resentment regarding the favors or blessings of another person. The true meaning of envy is the desire of a blessing, a virtue, the self-sufficiency of a person disappearing, whether the jealous one aspires this for himself or not, is resentment of another person possessing this favor. In fact, to the extent that if he was told "Let him keep it, we will give the same to you also" he would not be satisfied, such a person would be happy not to be given anything, just as long as the other person is deprived of what he possesses. In particular, if this resented blessing is a personal virtue that is impossible for the envious one to obtain, then he becomes an outright enemy of the bearer of these virtues, and because he is not able to acquire this blessing himself, this individual will certainly attempt to find consolation in unjustly destroying the one against whom he feels jealousy. "May Allah forbid!"

As a summary, the envier does not pursue his own interests, but wants the evil of the person he envies. When a person has the desire of owning or being like the possessor of that blessing or virtue, but does not resent a possession of virtue of another person, then this is not classified as jealousy, but is envy which harbors no evil. It was reported that a believer experiences envy bearing no evil, whereas a hypocrite experiences jealousy. The jealous are the ones who are despised by Allah, and by the servants of Allah. Jealousy is also noted as one of the greatest sins. As for jealousy by nature, if one who struggles to oppress and does not act upon this emotion, but treats his fellow believer in a manner which pleases Allah, then this is not classified as a sin. Maybe this person who is jealous by nature will be granted reward because he suppressed his emotions of jealousy and treated his fellow believer with kindness. Certainly, it is quite clear that a person who bears a characteristic by nature experiences great difficulty in resisting its effects.

Envy is when a person wants to possess a blessing or characteristic of another individual, but without the other person losing those blessings, there is no harm in this. Indeed, this is the meaning of this tradition of the Prophet: "Envy is not permissible but in two cases: A man to whom Allah has granted wealth and he disposes of it on the path of truth, and a man to whom Allah granted knowledge and he acts upon this and teaches it to others."[46]

Even though *hasad* usually defines jealousy, it is what is more commonly known as "ghayrat" in Arabic. Indeed, as the famous translator Asim Efendi said: "*Ghayrat, ghayr, ghar, ghiyar*: means guarding from situations which may shame ones reputation or honor, and this is called jealousy." For example, a man being jealous of his wife, or a woman being jealous of her husband is not jealousy with evil intent, this is *ghayrat* (literally meaning a person not wanting to share his rights with others), an act which is

---

[46] *Sahih al-Bukhari*, Zakah, 5

praised. However, when a person is jealous of another person's wife, husband, wealth, beauty or is intolerant and desires of the elimination of any blessing, quality or honor of another individual this is jealousy, and this was detested. Jealousy and envy with evil intent was detested whereas *ghayrat*, the kind of jealousy mentioned earlier is a characteristic that is approved and praised.

Say: I seek refuge in the Lord of the daybreak from the evil mentioned. Seek refuge in Allah the Self-Sufficient, the Eternal because He is the Creator of all and is the only One who can protect from all evil, and those who seek refuge in Him with sincerity have been promised His protection; "… *Allah is the Best as protector, and He is the Most Merciful of the merciful*" (Yusuf 12:64).

After saying I seek refuge in Allah from "the evil of what He has created," seeking refuge in Him from other things is an indication of the extent of the evil of that from which refuge is sought. Lastly, by seeking refuge "from the evil of the envious one when he envies," this signifies that the evil of the jealous and envious is a greater evil. As jealousy was the first reason in the heavens and the earth for rebelling against Allah. Iblis rebelled against the command of Allah because of his jealousy of Adam. Qabil (Cain) killed his brother Habil (Abel) because of his jealousy.

SURAH AN-NAS

بِسْمِ اللهِ الرَّحْمٰنِ الرَّحِيمِ

قُلْ أَعُوذُ بِرَبِّ النَّاسِ ۞ مَلِكِ النَّاسِ ۞ إِلٰهِ النَّاسِ ۞ مِنْ شَرِّ الْوَسْوَاسِ

الْخَنَّاسِ ۞ الَّذِي يُوَسْوِسُ فِي صُدُورِ النَّاسِ ۞ مِنَ الْجِنَّةِ وَالنَّاسِ ۞

Interpretation

In the Name of Allah, the All-Merciful, the All-Compassionate,

1. Say: I seek refuge in the Lord of humankind,
2. The Sovereign of humankind,
3. The Deity of humankind,
4. From the evil of the sneaking whisperer (the Satan),
5. Who whispers into the hearts of humankind,
6. Of the jinn and humankind.

The surah, which takes its name from the word "nas" repeated at the end of the verses meaning humankind, consists of six verses. It is a continuation of the previous Surah al-Falaq, and commands to seek the refuge of Allah from the whispers of mankind and jinn.

Commentary

1. قُلْ أَعُوذُ بِرَبِّ النَّاسِ *"Say: 'I seek refuge in the Lord of human-kind.'"*

As in Surah al-Falaq, this surah also begins with "I seek refuge" mentioning three of the attributes of Allah, and commands to seek refuge in

Him. The first being Allah, "The Lord of humankind," the One who Sustains, the Nurturer and Master of humankind. The second "The Sovereign of humankind"; Allah the King, the Ruler of humankind. The third is "The Deity of humankind"; the one and only Allah, Deity of humankind.

In the Qur'an the word "ilah" (deity) is used in two meanings. The first is an individual or thing that is worshipped although it is not a deity. The second, is the Deity that must be worshipped, and whether He is worshipped or not, He is the One Allah. Wherever the word "ilah" is used regarding Allah, it is used in the second form.

Despite the fact that Allah is the Lord of the whole creation, it was not enough that He repeated the word "nas" (humankind) three times to honor and dignify humans, to manifest their honor, value and signify that they are held in high esteem. In addition, Allah also honored humans in this way: He granted everything in the universe as a favor to mankind, and granted them intelligence and knowledge to sustain them; He commanded His angels to prostrate before mankind. So mankind is certainly the most superior of all creation.

2. مَلِك النَّاس *"The Sovereign of humankind"*

In other words, I seek refuge in the Sovereign of mankind, the One who nurtures and educates, who governs with His rules with the commands in accordance with knowledge and reason. Obviously, this is not the temporal ruler or sovereign that we know, this is seeking refuge in the Sovereign, the Lord who grants wealth and sovereignty to whom He wills, the One who can take this wealth and sovereignty away from whom He wills, the One who has the power to destroy whom He wills as revealed in this verse "*O Allah, absolute Master of all dominion! You give dominion to whom You will, and take away dominion from whom You will, and You exalt and honor whom You will, and abase whom You will; in Your hand is all good; surely You have full power over everything*" (Al Imran 3:26).

According to certain scholars, the reason for Allah commanding: " (say I seek refuge)in the Lord of humankind, in the Sovereign of humankind and in the Deity of humankind," is because there are rulers and kings among humans. So Allah is revealing that He is their Lord and ruler. In addition, there are also those who worship other rulers and so called deities from among themselves. Due to this, Allah also announced that He is their Lord and Deity, that they must worship Him and not their kings or leaders.

3. إِلَهِ النَّاسِ *"The Deity of humankind"*

I seek refuge in the true, the only Allah of mankind; in the Deity to whom all who are sane, who have reached maturity are accountable for their faith and worship: the One has the power to create and command, to give and take life, to sustain and destroy, to reward and punish, the One and only Allah, the Self-Sufficient, the Eternal.

As we can now see, the previous surah only mentions one attribute in which to seek refuge *"The Lord of the daybreak,"* whereas the evil of that created by Allah, and from which refuge is to be sought were classified as three: The darkness (*ghasiq*), blowing (*naffathat*) and envy (*hasad*). In this surah, three attributes are mentioned in which refuge must be sought "Rabbi'n-nas, Maliki'n-nas, Ilahi'n-nas," whereas there is only one evil from which refuge must be sought. Therefore, this evil, this calamity is greater, more threatening than all. We must classify guarding against this as the one of the most important objectives throughout *every* stage of a person's life, and in particular during the final stage of life.

The Lord, Sovereign and Deity are three attributes of Allah the Almighty. He is the Lord, the Sovereign, the Deity of everything. Everything is His creation and His servant. Therefore, those who seek refuge were commanded to seek refuge in the One who possesses these attributes alone.

4. مِنْ شَرِّ الْوَسْوَاسِ الْخَنَّاسِ *"From the evil of the sneaking whisperer (the Satan)"*

I seek refuge from the evil of that treacherous, that devious, that regressive source of provocation and the whispers that entice to evil and withdraw.

Waswas, which actually means prompter of evil suggestions or scheming deceiver, was used here as a title, a name, the same *waswas* can in a sense can mean to define the source of deceit and evil. "Al-waswas" was also one of the names of Satan. Indeed, the devil's sole pursuit and talent is whispering evil suggestions and enticing people from the true path.

Here the word "waswas'il-khannas" was used. The meaning of "waswas" is the "one who repeatedly whispers evil." Whereas the meaning of *waswasa* is to repeatedly whisper evil suggestions into a person's heart without him even realizing. The word *waswas* suggests the repeating, recurrence of an act, as in the case of "zalzalah" (earthquake). As attempting to provoke a person only once would be insufficient. Such an action is called "waswasa" and the one who entices or tempts is called "waswas."

As for the word "khannas," it is the present participle of "khunus" or in connection with this, is an attribute of *waswas*. This means repeating the act in question frequently. Here, it is clear that the one who whispers these evil suggestions returns to a person frequently. When the word *al-khannas* is added, it means: the one who whispers and retreats, one who comes repeatedly in an attempt of enticing the person with his whispers. In other words; when he is unsuccessful the first time, the one who returns for a second, third or fourth attempt to lure with his evil whispers. As a majority of scholars agree "waswas'il-khannas" means the devil.

So what is *waswasa*? *Waswasa* means to whisper gently, to whisper in secret. Inspirations of evil, in other words the evil or harmful thoughts conveyed into the heart from the soul or by the devil, and the whispers of confusion and deceit. The verse "*...it is We Who have created human, and We know what suggestions his soul makes to him*" (Qaf 50:16) refers to the whispers of the soul, whereas the verse "*But Satan made an evil suggestion, saying: "O Adam..."*" (Ta-Ha 20:120) refers to the evil whispers of the devil.

Here, there is an indication that these whispers entice acts of evil. Inspirations of evil initially have an effect on the blind and heedless individuals, and this generates evil desires in the heart. Then this evil intention transforms into a command, and with the effects of these evil suggestions, the command becomes more dominant. As a result, an evil act emerges.

The meaning of seeking refuge in Allah from that which whispers these evil suggestions is to eliminate that evil from the very beginning.

If we approach this from another angle, the attempts of those who incite these evil inspirations can be categorized as: the incitements such as disbelief, polytheism and atheism that encourage disobedience towards Allah and His Messenger, and that which entices hostility towards believers. If these incitements are unsuccessful, and the individual is not deceived by this provocation and embraces Islam, then the devil begins to encourage the practice of innovations in Islam, whispering inspirations that there is no harm in this. Thus, the devil and his accomplices hope that the accumulation of trivial sins will transform into major sins. If they are unsuccessful in this also, then they strive to confine belief to the individual in question and make him prevail over the other believers. If that person is not deceived regardless of all these attempts, then the devil and his accomplices mount an attack, and provoke all the people and jinn against him. At this point, the devil comes to the believer and says "By tolerating this, you are displaying your cowardliness. You must revolt against them." This is the devils last weapon. By doing this, the devil is striving to misguide those who call others to the path of Allah, and wants to incite the person to failure in his cause. If the devil is unsuccessful yet again and escapes these evil traps, then the devil is powerless.

In order to eliminate any reservations regarding what "waswas'il-khannas" is, this explanation was given, the one:

5. اَلَّذِي يُوَسْوِسُ فِي صُدُورِ النَّاسِ **"Who whispers into the hearts of humankind"**

Various forms of evil suggestions are released into the souls of humans; whether this is in the souls, in the hearts of individuals, or whether it is in the souls as societies, and into the hearts of those who are unmindful of Allah from the inner and exterior senses to the minds, into the hearts whether perceived or unperceived, gradually prompting evil, arousing evil inclinations and despicable emotions. In this way, these inspirations deviates the mind and thoughts, and entice to all kinds of evil.

These whispers prevent a person from pursuing the path of Allah and reaching the purpose of humanity, eventually leading to disbelief and to eternal destruction. So "waswas'il-khannas," is whatever repeatedly whispers the enticements, the source of evil, into the hearts of the heedless.

6. مِنَ الْجِنَّةِ وَالنَّاسِ *"Of the jinn and humankind"*

In other words, whether that which conveys these whispers are jinn from the unseen body of jinn, or whether it is by people from among mankind, "waswas'il-khannas" applies to both.

There are two kinds of whisperers who whisper evil into the hearts of humans: the first is from among the unseen group of existence from the metaphysical realm, the jinn, and the others are those from among the visible and familiar existence, humans. This is mentioned in Surah al-An'am: *"And thus it is that We have set against every Prophet a hostile opposition from among the Satans of humankind and jinn, whispering and suggesting to one another specious words, by way of delusion"* (al-An'am 6:112) in accordance with this meaning, it declares in general the whisperer can be from the devils of the jinn and mankind, so therefore it is necessary to seek refuge in Allah from the evil of the whispers of all.

Everyone possesses a devil that attempts to misguide him to evil and displays evil acts to be attractive and appealing. The Prophet said: "Every one of you has been assigned a companion from the jinn. The Companions asked: Even you O Messenger of Allah?" The noble Prophet replied: "Even me, except that Allah has helped me against him and he has submitted. Now he only tells me to do good."[47]

This last verse of the Qur'an teaches us to protect ourselves form the evil of the whole of humanity and the jinn. Undoubtedly, the devils of humans are a greater threat, more fatal than the devils of jinn. Because when refuge is sought in Allah, the devils of the jinn hide, whereas the devils of humans display evil to be good and appealing, and entice to evil. Nothing

---

[47] *Darimi*, Riqaq, 25; Ahmad ibn Hanbal, *Musnad*, I/385

can persuade such a person to desist from his determination. The innocent and harmless are only those protected by Allah.

There are three cures against the whispers of the devil: The first is mentioning and remembering Allah frequently, the second is seeking His refuge frequently and the most beneficial of this is reciting this surah. The third is resisting the devil with great determination, and acting to the contrary of what the devil commands.

Indeed, it was commanded to seek the refuge of the Lord of humankind, the Sovereign of humankind and the Deity of humankind from the all evil, and in particular from the evil of the devil's whispers, and those who seek refuge in this manner are assured that they will be protected by the help of Allah, and beginning by reciting al-Fatiha is the greatest display of praise and appreciation: *"All praise and gratitude are for Allah, the Lord of the worlds"* (al-Fatiha 1:2).

If we count the letters of this sublime surah, there are twenty two unrepeated letters (including the prolonging letters). The letters in al-Fatiha are the same. This is an extremely meaningful coincidence, and indicates that there is a close connection between the beginning and the end of the Qur'an in terms of meaning, and indeed in other aspects.

Another interesting point regarding al-Mu'awwidhatayn or the Verses of Refuge (Surahs al-Falaq and an-Nas) is the relation between the beginning and the end of the Qur'an. The Qur'an was not compiled according to the occasion of the revelation of the verses. The order of the verses of the Qur'an, which were revealed over a period of twenty three years in various places according to the period, conditions and requirements was not arranged by the Prophet, but on the command of Allah who revealed these verses. According to this order, the Qur'an begins with Surah al-Fatiha and ends with the Verses of Refuge. When believers are heedful of these two verses; after praising and glorifying Allah, the All-Merciful, the All-Compassionate, the Master of the Day of Judgment, the servant says: O Lord! You alone do I worship, and to You alone do I ask for help. What I need from You is Your guidance… In response to this, Allah gave His servants the

Qur'an as guidance to the path of truth. Allah, the Lord of the daybreak, the Lord of humankind, the Sovereign of humankind and the Deity of humankind commands His servants to supplicate: "I seek refuge in You alone from the evil and mischief of all creatures, and in particular from the whisperings of the devils from among men and jinn, as they are the greatest obstacles on the path of truth.

And lastly, there is rhythmic harmony in this surah, its excellence is impossible to describe. Its beauty can only be truly perceived when recited in Arabic, its original form. In this verse it commands seeking refuge from the jinn and humans, and from those who approach deceitfully and whisper evil suggestions and thoughts. The topic here is regarding is inspiring evil thoughts with whispers. So we will now read the surah in Arabic:

بِسْمِ اللهِ الرَّحْمٰنِ الرَّحِيمِ

قُلْ أَعُوذُ بِرَبِّ النَّاسِ ۞ مَلِكِ النَّاسِ ۞ إِلٰهِ النَّاسِ ۞ مِنْ شَرِّ الْوَسْوَاسِ الْخَنَّاسِ ۞ الَّذِي يُوَسْوِسُ فِي صُدُورِ النَّاسِ ۞ مِنَ الْجِنَّةِ وَالنَّاسِ ۞

Can you sense the sound of whispering in your ear? The "s" on the end of the words echoes a whisper in the ear. Indeed, this is how the Qur'an is, not only does it convey the meaning of the words, but also recreates the subject with its utterance and harmonic tones. It explains the subject with words that provide sounds consistent with its content. Glory be to Allah the Almighty!

SOURCES

Akgül, Muhittin, *Kur'an-ı Kerim'de Hz. Peygamber*, Işık Yayınları, Istanbul. 2004.

_____, "Toplumu Islahta Kur'an'ın Öngördüğü Bazı İlkeler," *Diyanet İlmi Dergi*, v. 34, no. 1, 1998.

Albayrak, Halis, *Vahiy Gerçeği*, (Kutlu Doğum Haftası, 1989), DVY, Ankara, 1990.

Asqalani, Ibn Hajar Ahmad ibn Ali, *Al-Matalibu'l-Aliya*, Daru'l-Ma'rifa, Beirut, nd.

Aydemir, Abdullah, "Mensuh Âyetler," *Diyanet Dergisi*, December 1988.

Bakr Ismail, *Dirasat fi Ulumi'l-Qur'an*, Daru'l-Manar, Cairo, 1991.

Bayhaqi, Abu Bakr Ahmad ibn Husayn, *Dalailu'n-Nubuwwa*, Beirut, 1985.

Bilmen, Ömer Nasuhi, *Büyük Tefsir Tarihi*, Bilmen Yayınevi, Istanbul, 1973.

Bucaille, Maurice, *Le Bible, Le Coran et Le Science*, Seghers Publishers, Paris, 1977.

al-Bukhari, Abu Abdillah Muhammad ibn Ismail, *Al-Jami'u's-Sahih*, Al-Maktabatu'l-Islamiyya, Istanbul, nd.

Buti, Muhammad Said Ramadan, *Allah'ın Kitabında İki Harika Olay*, Kur'an'ı Anlamada Çağdaş Bir Yaklaşım: Risale-i Nur Örneği, Uluslar Arası Bediüzzaman Sempozyumu 4.

Cerrahoğlu, İsmail, *Tefsir Usulü*, Ankara, 1979.

Demirci, Muhsin, *Vahiy Gerçeği*, İFAV, Istanbul, 1996.

Drad, Muhammad A. *En Mühim Mesaj Kur'an*, (tr. Suat Yıldırım), Akçağ Yayınları, Ankara, 1985.

Elmalılı, M. Hamdi Yazır, *Hak Dini Kur'an Dili*, Azim Dağıtım, Istanbul, nd.

Firuzabadi, *Al-Qamusu'l-Muhit*, Muassasatu'r-Risala, Beirut, 1993.

Gülen, M. Fethullah, *Fatiha Üzerine Mülahazalar*, Nil Yayınları, İzmir, 2001.

_____, *Yeşeren Düşünceler*, Nil Yayınları, İzmir, 1999.

_____, *Vuslat Muştusu*, Nil Yayınları, İzmir, 2008.

Harman, Ö. Faruk, *G.A*, Istanbul, 1977.

Haythami, Nuraddin Ali ibn Abi Bakr, *Majmau'z-Zawaid wa Manbau'l-Fawaid*, Daru'r-Rayyan, Cairo, 1987.

Ibn Faris, Abu'l-Husayn Ahmad ibn Faris ibn Zakariyya, *Mu'jamu'l-Maqayis fi'l-Lugha*, Daru'l-Fikr, Beirut, 1994.

Ibn Hanbal, Ahmad, *Musnad*, Beirut, nd.

Ibn Hisham, *As-Siratu'n-Nabawiyya*, Dar al-Ihyai't-Turasi'l-Arabi, Egypt, nd.

Ibn Qayyim al-Jawziyya, Shamsuddin Abu Abdillah, *At-Tibyan fi Ulumi'l-Qur'an*, Daru'l-Kutubi'l-Ilmiyya, Beirut, 1982.

Ibn Sa'd, *At-Tabaqatu'l-Kubra*, Dar al-Sadr, Beirut, nd.

Isbahani, Abu Nuaym, *Dalailu'n-Nubuwwa*, Daru'n-Nafais, Beirut, 1991.

Jawhari, Ismail ibn Hammad, *Sihah*, Cairo, 1950.

Jurjani, Abdul Qahir, *Asraru'l-Balagha,* Daru'l-Matba'ati'l-Arabiyya, nd.

Jurjani, Sharif Ali ibn Muhammad, *At-Ta'rifat*, Daru'l-Kutubi'l-Ilmiyya, Beirut, 1988.

Kattan, Manna, *Mabahis fi Ulumi'l-Qur'an*, Maktabatu'l-Ma'arif, Riyad, 1988.

Kutup, Muhammed, *Yirminci Asrın Cahiliyeti*, (tr. M. Hasan Beşer), Cağaloğlu Yayınevi, Istanbul, 1971.

Mahmud, Mustafa, *Kur'an'a Yeni Yaklaşımlar*, (tr. Muhittin Akgül), IşıkYayınları, Istanbul, 2004.

Mustafa Muslim, *Mabahis fi I'jazi'l-Qur'an*, Daru'l-Muslim, Riyad, 1996

Nadwi, Abu'l-Hasan Ali al-Hasani, *Kitap ve Sünnetin Işığında Dört Rukün*, (tr. İsmet Ersöz), İslami Neşriyat, Konya, 1991.

Nadwi, Sulayman, *Ar-Risalatu'l-Muhammadiyya*, Daru's-Suudiyye, Jeddah, 1984.

Nasafi, Abdullah ibn Ahmad ibn Mahmud, *Madariku't-Tanzil,* Daru'l-Kutubi'l-Ilmiyya, Beirut, 1995.

Nursi, Bediüzzaman, *Sözler*, Tenvir Neşriyat, Istanbul, nd.

Okiç, M. Tayyib, *Tefsir ve Hadis Usulünün Bazı Meseleleri*, Nun Yayıncılık, Istanbul, 1995.

Qadi Iyad, Abu'l-Fadl al-Yahsubi, *Ash-Shifa bi Ta'rif-i Hukuki'l-Mustafa*, Daru'l-Fikr, Beirut, 1988.

Qutub, Sayyid, *Fi Zilali'l-Qur'an*, Daru'sh-Shuruq, Beirut, 1988.

Rafii, Mustafa Sadiq, *I'jazu'l-Qur'an*, Beirut, 1973.

Ragib al-Isfahani, *Al-Mufradat,* Beirut, nd.

Salih, Subhi, *Hadis İlimleri ve Hadis Istılahları*, (tr. M. Yaşar Kandemir), Diyanet İşleri Başkanlığı Yayınları, Ankara, 1986.

_____, *Mabahis fi Ulumi'l-Qur'an*, Dersaadet, Istanbul, nd.

Suyuti, Jalaluddin Abdurrahman, *Al-Itqan fi Ulumi'l-Qur'an*, Dar-u Ibn-Kathir, Beirut, 1987.

_____, *Asbab an-Nuzul*, Dar'ul ibn Zakwan, Beirut, nd.

Shahhata, Abdullah Mahmud, *Ulumu'l-Qur'an*, Daru'l-I'tisam, Cairo, 1985.

Shibli, Mawlana, *Asr-ı Saadet,* (tr. Ömer Rıza Doğrul), Eser Neşriyat, Istanbul, 1978.

Shirbini, Hatib, *As-Siraju'l-Munir*, Daru'l-Ma'rifa, Beirut, nd.

Tabari, Ibn Jarir, *Jamiu'l-Bayan an Ta'wil'il-Ayi'l-Qur'an*, Daru'l-Fikr, Beirut, 1995.

Turgut, Ali, *Tefsir Usulü ve Kaynakları*, İFAV Yayınları, Istanbul,1991.

Ulutürk, Veli, "Kur'an'ın Muhafazası ve Yakılma Hadisesi," *Yeni Ümit*, no. 6, 7, 8, 9.

Wahidi, Abu'l-Hasan Ali ibn Ahmad an-Nisaburi, *Asbab an-Nuzul*, Daru'l-Islah, Dammam, 1991.

Yardım, Ali, *Hadis I*, Dokuz Eylül Üniversitesi Yayınları, İzmir, 1984.

Yavuz, Yunus Vehbi, *İslamda Zekat Müessesesi*, Çağrı Yayınları, Istanbul, 1983.

Yekta Saraç, M. A., *Klasik Edebiyat Bilgisi Belagat*, Bilimevi, Istanbul, 2000.

Yıldırım, Suat, *Kur'an-ı Kerim ve Kur'an İlimlerine Giriş*, Ensar Neşriyat, nd.

———, *Peygamberimizin Kur'an'ı Tefsiri,* Yeni Akademi Yayınları, Istanbul, 2006.

Zabidi, Zaynu'd-din Ahmad ibn Ahmad ibn Abdi'l-Latif, *Sahih-i Buhari Muhtasarı, Tecrid-i Sarih Tercemesi*, (tr. Ahmed Naim), D.İ.B.Y, Ankara, 1984.

Zarqani, Muhammad Abdul Adhim, *Manahilu'l-Irfan fi Ulumi'l-Qur'an*, Daru'l-Kutubi'l-Ilmiyya, Beirut, 1988.

Zarkashi, Badruddin Muhammad ibn Abdullah, *Al-Burhan fi Ulumi'l-Qur'an*, Daru'l-Ma'rifa, Beirut, nd.